MW01138824

"One of the things I love about these books is that they are so accessible to every aspiring writer."

— RICK LUDWIG, AUTHOR OF *MIRRORED*

"I reread these books before I start each book I write."

— CALLIE HUTTON, *USA TODAY*-BESTSELLING AUTHOR OF *FOR THE LOVE OF THE VISCOUNT*

"Bernhardt shows you exactly what makes literary characters keep people interested and how to use those strengths when creating characters of your own."

— R.J. JOHNSON, AUTHOR OF *THE TWELVE STONES*

"Easy to read while delivering good material with some occasional humor."

— DAVID SULLIVAN, AUTHOR

"This book gives everything that it promises. And all the other writing books written by William Bernhardt are on my wish list."

— C.H. SCARLETT, AUTHOR

WHAT WRITERS NEED TO KNOW

Essential Topics

WILLIAM BERNHARDT

BABYLON
BOOKS

Dedicated to all the Red Sneaker Writers:
You cannot fail if you refuse to quit.

"A professional writer is an amateur who didn't quit."

— RICHARD BACH

CONTENTS

INTRODUCTION

If this is not your first Red Sneaker book, or if you've attended Red Sneaker retreats or conventions, you can skip to Chapter One. If you're new, let me take a moment to explain.

I've been telling stories for several decades, doing almost every kind of writing imaginable. I've been speaking at workshops and conferences almost as long. Every time I step behind the podium I see long rows of talented people frustrated by the fact that they haven't sold any books. Yes, the market is changing and agents are hard to find and self-publishing can be challenging. But when aspiring writers work hard but still don't succeed...there's usually a reason. Too often enormous potential is lost due to a lack of fundamental knowledge. Sometimes a little guidance is all that stands between an unknown writer and a satisfying writing career.

I've seen writing instructors and writing texts that seem more interested in appearing literary than in providing useful information. Sometimes I think presenters do more to obfuscate the subject than to explain it. Perhaps they feel that if they make the writing process as mysterious as possible, it will make them seem profound—or perhaps they don't understand the subject well themselves. Some of the best writers I know are not particularly good teachers, because they've never thought consciously about the creative process.

Hoping to be more useful, I founded the Red Sneaker Writing Center. Why Red Sneakers? Because I love my red sneakers. They're practical, flexible, sturdy—full of flair and fun. In other words, they're exactly what writing instruction should be. Practical, dynamic, and designed to unleash the creative spirit, to give the imagination a platform for creating wondrous work.

I held the first Red Sneaker Writers conference in 2005. I invited the best speakers I knew, people who had published many books but also could teach. Then I launched my small-group writing retreats—intensive days working with a handful of aspiring writers. The retreats gave me the opportunity to read, edit, and work one-on-one with people so I could target their needs and make sure they got what would help them most. This approach worked well and I'm proud to say a substantial number of writers have graduated from my programs, published, and even hit the bestseller lists. But of course, not everyone can attend a retreat.

This book, and the others in this series, are designed to provide assistance to writers regardless of their location. The books are short, inexpensive, and targeted to specific areas where a writer might want help.

Let me see if I can anticipate your questions:

Why are these books so short? Because I've expunged the unnecessary and the unhelpful. I've pared it down to the essential information, useful ideas that can improve the quality of your writing. Too many instructional books are padded with excerpts and repetition to fill word counts required by book contracts. That's not the Red Sneaker way.

Why are you writing several different books instead of one big book? I encourage writers to commit to writing every day and to maintain a consistent writing schedule. Sometimes reading about writing can be an excuse for not writing. You can read the Red Sneaker books without losing much time. In fact, each can be read in an afternoon. Take one day off from your writing. Make notes as you read. See if that doesn't trigger ideas about how you might improve your writing. Then get back to work.

You reference other books as examples, but you rarely quote excerpts. Why?

Two reasons. First, I'm trying to keep these books brief. I will cite a book as an example, and if you want to look up a particular passage, it's easy enough to do. You don't need me to cut and paste it for you. Second, if I quote from materials currently under copyright protection, I have to pay a fee, which means I'd need to raise the price of the book. I don't want to do that. I think you can grasp my points without reading copyrighted excerpts. Too often, in my opinion, excessive excerpting is done to pad the page count.

Why does each chapter end with exercises?

The exercises are a completely integrated and essential part of the book, designed to simulate what happens in my small-group writing retreats. Samuel Johnson was correct when he wrote: *Scribendo disces scribere.* Meaning: You learn to write by writing. These principles won't be concretized in your brain until you put them into practice.

So get the full benefit from this book. Complete the exercises. If you were in one of my retreats, this would be your homework. I won't be hovering over your shoulder as you read this book— but you should do the exercises anyway.

What else does the Red Sneaker Writers Center do?

We send out a free e-newsletter filled with writing advice, market analysis, and other items of interest. If you would like to be added to the mailing list, please visit my website. We also have a free bi-weekly Red Sneaker podcast with all the latest news and interviews with industry professionals. I host an annual conference, WriterCon, over Labor Day weekend and small-group writing retreats throughout the year. There will be future books in this series. And we sponsor a literary magazine called *Conclave* that would love to see you submit your poems, short fiction, and creative nonfiction. Our Balkan Press publishes books, primarily fiction and poetry.

Okay, enough of the warm-up act. Read this book. Then write your story. Follow your dreams. Never give up.

William Bernhardt

CREATING A MEMORABLE SERIES CHARACTER

"Think of your character as a jewel that has about a thousand different facets. If you keep turning them over and exploring new sides, you'll keep discovering new information about their personality and motivations."

— LAUREN SAPALA

Thirty years passed between when I created Ben Kincaid and when I created my current series character, Daniel Pike. Trying to come up with a new protagonist who would sustain at least six books caused me to think long and hard about what makes a durable series character readers like enough to revisit.

The first time around, I didn't do this. Ben Kincaid was originally intended to be the protagonist of one novel: *The Fixed Moment*. (The publisher retitled it *Primary Justice*. I still don't know what that means.) Series characters were less prevalent then, and it might have been presumptuous of me to imagine I was launching a series since I'd never published anything, despite years of trying and hundreds of rejection letters. My beloved editor, Joe Blades, said he thought this guy could lead a series—and that's what happened, for nineteen books (so far). Even when I later created Susan Pulaski, I was only thinking of a single book (*Dark Eye*), with more psychological depth and heartache than the typical thriller.

But now I'm older and I pretend to be wiser, so I've taken a somewhat more systematic approach. I looked at all the great series characters out there, like Steve Berry's Cotton Malone and Ben Aaronovitch's Peter Grant. I even looked at series books from previous eras, like Anthony Trollope's Barchester books (which I recently completed reading and feel quite virtuous for having done so). What makes a series work? I asked myself. What brings readers back, book after book? I was enthusiastic about my lead character, Daniel Pike—but how could I inspire readers to feel the same?

Based upon this inquiry, I'm offering suggestions on creating durable series characters. I assume you will instill your project with all the essential elements of good storytelling (and if you're not sure what those are, reread those Red Sneaker books). But what does the main character need to succeed?

Here's what I came up with. Call it the series character checklist:

1) Give the character something that makes him/her special.

This doesn't have to be a flat-out superpower, but something distinctive, so the character isn't just another lawyer, doctor, PI, cop, wizard, etc. The paradigm, of course, is Sherlock Holmes, whose inductive reasoning abilities allowed him to solve complex puzzles. I gave Daniel Pike something similarly cognitive, but more related to the work of a lawyer. He has the ability to make careful observations of the people he encounters—which often allows him to discern hidden truths. Sometimes he gets it simply by watching people, uncovering liars. Sometimes it's by combining observations in meaningful and unexpected ways.

Sometimes it's pure instinct. But it's a power most lawyers don't have (trust me) and I thought it would not only make Dan a miracle worker in the courtroom—but a delight to watch in action.

2) Give the character something that makes him/her fun.

First and foremost, I gave Dan a sense of humor. At times, it's a bit acerbic, but he's never boring. I thought if he made readers laugh, they were bound to like him more. His success as a lawyer has led to a first-class lifestyle (a complete contrast to Ben Kincaid), a fondness for gourmet cooking, extreme sports, and fast cars. All fun stuff to read about, right? Some of Dan's recipes should make your mouth water—and they are all dishes I've made myself. Yes, I include recipes in the back of the book.

3) Give the character something that makes him/her quirky.

Daniel's a rebel. Though with a big law firm when the first book starts, he's not part of the corporate culture. He lives on a boat—because why not?—he wears Air Jordans in court, and he carries a backpack rather than a briefcase. I mean, honestly, doesn't that make more sense? I don't understand why people don't wear sneakers every day. And backpacks are much easier on the shoulders. Making your series characters eccentric or unusual will enhance their memorability. You want to give the reader something to hold onto, so when the next book in the series rolls around, they think, Oh yeah, he's the guy in the sneakers...

4) Give the character something he/she's passionate about.

Shannon Adler once wrote, "If you want to discover the true character of a person, you have only to observe what they are passionate about." I agree. Daniel Pike is passionate about justice, and not as an abstract concept but as a reality he fights for in the courtroom. He likes making money, sure, but his primary drive is preventing people from being railroaded by the government. He has a personal reason for feeling so strongly about this. He believes that most people are presumed guilty and prosecutors have a devastating ability to put people away regardless of their guilt. He refuses to let the government destroy people's lives. This is the driving force behind his career, behind every case he accepts. To him, it's not about whether his clients are good or bad people. He will fight to see that justice is done.

If you can give your character those four critical qualities, you'll have someone capable of carrying a series. And this is a good time to do it. Series books have never been more popular. Publishers see series books as the safest bet they can make. Readers enjoy revisiting characters they love. It's a win-win, if you can bring it off. But it all starts with creating the right character.

HIGHLIGHTS/EXERCISES

Highlights

1) Series characters are more popular than ever.

2) Give your series characters something that makes them special.

3) Give your series characters something that makes them fun.

4) Give your series characters something that makes them quirky.

5) Give your series characters something they are passionate about.

6) Create a character you enjoy spending time with.

Red Sneaker Exercises

1) Who are the series characters you have most enjoyed over the

course of your reading life? What characters have maintained their places in your heart? What character would you be willing to read about again, regardless of the plot? Now ask yourself what about this character appeals to you. Can you get some of that into the character you're creating?

2) When devising your character's gift, special talent, or super-power, think about the kind of story you are writing. You want to give your character a special ability that will be useful in the plots you devise throughout the series. Being a dog whisperer is nice, but probably not that helpful when trying to solve a mystery. I have great admiration for people who crochet, but I don't see that helping much in an outer-space SF adventure. Can you give your character an ability that helps explain why, book after book, they are the one who prevails?

3) The fact that you will use a character in multiple books does not mean the character cannot have character arcs. We all go on many journeys during the course of our life. You can find a unique one for each volume in the saga. This does mean, though, that it may be useful to start when a character is at an early point in their life, career, or emotional development. You want them to have someplace to go, some way to mature or evolve, over the course of many adventures. What would be the best starting point for your series character's "big picture" journey?

SHOULD YOU WRITE IN THE FIRST PERSON?

"The most fatal illusion is the settled point of view. Since life is growth and motion, a fixed point of view kills anybody who has one."

— BROOKS ATKINSON

Every writer starting a new project must make fundamental decisions about viewpoint. First person or third person? (Let's leave second person to academics unconcerned about sales.) Single viewpoint or multiple viewpoint? And your answers to these questions should be based upon your understanding that:

1) they are not the same question, and

2) you should do what's best for the story you're telling.

First person, of course, means that one of the characters, who may be the protagonist, uses first-person pronouns and speaks directly to the reader: "Last night I dreamt I went to Manderley again." The first-person narrator is typically the central character but doesn't have to be. Nick Carraway narrates *The Great Gatsby*, but I think the titular Gatz is the big cheese. This is not the same as deciding whether to have multiple viewpoints. Many first-person novels, like *Gatsby*, are told entirely from a single viewpoint. Others, like my *Dark Eye*, are told primarily in first person by the protagonist, but switch periodically to a third-person antagonist. Many other recent thrillers have used the same approach.

In my Ben Kincaid series, I wrote the first eighteen books in third person, but for the nineteenth, *Justice Returns*, I used first-person Ben as narrator (though I occasionally jumped to other viewpoints presented as interview transcripts incorporated into Ben's record). This helped me energize the story and make it seem fresh rather than yet another iteration of the same book. I'm not sure any of my readers even noticed. I have yet to see this change in perspective mentioned in a single review. Which may lead us to another conclusion: If you write it well, these technical details that writers obsess over may be largely invisible to the reader.

So you have many mix-and-match options. Which should you employ? In my writing retreats I have noticed a tendency for many first-time writers to choose first-person narration. I can see why this might seem appealing. On the surface, it might look simpler, more obtainable. (Indeed, the earliest examples of English novels—*Robinson Crusoe*, *Pamela*, and *Joseph Andrews*—are all first person, possibly emulating the fake first-person confessions sold at public hangings in that era). If you're striving for reader-character intimacy, that is, to get readers inside your character's head, it seems like a natural approach. But there are three factors you need to understand before you write in first person, especially for a project as large as a novel:

1) **First person is not easier—it's harder.**

2) **First person has serious narrative limitations.**

3) **Some readers strongly dislike first-person narration.**

Let's take those in order. **First person is not easier.** It may seem so, especially if you imagine that the character's voice is your voice, perhaps the flashy, wisecracking, insightful superstar you see yourself as in your mind's eye, always one step ahead of the others and leaving the room with the perfect *esprit d'escalier* (the snappy comeback you think of an hour later while angrily reliving the scene in your head). But the truth is, no fictional character's voice is exactly the same as your voice, and even if it were, maintaining that voice consistently for eighty-thousand words would be a challenge. You must tell the entire story in a specific voice, and if it slips even for a moment, the reader will feel that something has gone wrong. I'm not saying it can't be done. I'm saying it's not something to attempt for your first book because you think it will be easier. I attempted first person for *Dark Eye*—after I'd been publishing for more than a decade.

First person has serious limitations. Anytime you write in viewpoint, you're restricted to what that character knows. But when you write an entire book from a single viewpoint, your narration is limited to what that viewpoint can see and hear. The novel *The Hunger Games* is told entirely from Katniss's viewpoint, but the film version broke from her viewpoint occasionally so the reader could see the riots breaking out while she was trapped in the game, or President Snow forming his evil plans while pruning his roses.

As I mentioned, you could write a hybrid first-person/third-person narrative. This creates page-turning suspense, because the reader learns something the protagonist does not know. Even then, however, the form has limitations. What if your narrator is not reliable? What if your protagonist is in denial about her problems (like Susan Pulaski in *Dark Eye*)? How will the reader figure it out? It's not impossible—you could reveal clues in a conversation with a trusted comrade, a dream sequence (ick!), a flashback (double-ick!), or some kind of external record, like a videotape or interview transcript (*Justice Returns*). But it's challenging.

Finally, you must realize that **some readers just can't tolerate**

first-person narration. I'm not sure why this is. It doesn't bother me, but I've heard others say a book loses all credibility once a character starts talking directly to them. Some moviegoers can't stand voiceover narration (mentioned in *The Opposite of Sex*) and I suspect it is much the same problem. Engaging readers in the fictional construct we call the novel requires a major suspension of disbelief. You have to lull readers' conscious minds into forgetting that these are just words on a page and lure them into a shared imaginary world. For some readers, when a character speaks directly to them, the illusion is shattered. It is much the same as when a movie character "breaks the fourth wall," that is, speaks directly to the camera (as in *Deadpool*, over and over again). Once the illusion is shattered, you'll probably never get it back.

First person is best used when you have a specific purpose for choosing that form. *Gatsby* uses it so we witness Nick's eventual disillusionment with the man he initially worships, which gives us insight into his dubious ideals, and implicitly, the dubious American Dream. *The Curious Incident of the Dog in the Night-time* uses first person to help us understand how an autistic youth thinks. In *The Murder of Roger Ackroyd*, Agatha Christie uses first person to deceive the reader and pull off one of the all-time great feats of misdirection. *Room* is narrated by a five-year old boy, a classic unreliable narrator who doesn't understand the horror of his situation. *Huckleberry Finn* uses an uneducated first-person narrator so the reader can witness his growing awareness of the deceit and inequity in the world.

I considered first-person narration for my latest series. I wanted to get readers into Daniel Pike's head fast, liking him and empathizing with him. I wanted readers to understand what drives this lawyer. But having him explain all this to the reader, or even remarking consciously upon it, seemed a bit of a cheat. I was convinced I could get the reader on board without alienating those who hate first person, or relinquishing the option of jumping to other viewpoints to generate mystery and suspense. Although the book is in Dan's viewpoint 90% of the time, I used occasional diversions to show the conspiracy growing and the threats to him personally, a tightening web he learns about long after the reader does. I made a conscious choice, after due deliberation, based upon the book itself and what I wanted to achieve.

None of this is intended to discourage you from writing whatever book you want to write. If you've got a first-person character voice desperate to get out, go for it. My goal, as always, is to have you make decisions based upon solid information, not misapprehensions. And there are some signs that first person may be gaining wider acceptance. It has become much more popular in young adult fiction. In the wake of *The Fault in Our Stars*, many YA books now feature first-person female teenage protagonists. I've seen it catching steam in the romance and SF fields as well. My bottom line advice is, first, that this may not be the best choice for early writers who will have many other problems to work through, and most importantly—don't attempt it unless you have a good reason.

HIGHLIGHTS/EXERCISES

Highlights

1) First-person narration means one of the characters uses first-person pronouns and speaks directly to the reader.

2) You can use a single viewpoint character or multiple viewpoints, regardless of whether you write in first person or third person.

3) Your viewpoint choices should be based upon what's best for your story.

4) First-person narration is not easier—it's harder.

5) First-person narration has serious limitations.

6) Some readers dislike first-person narration.

7) First-person narration may be a challenging choice for a first-time writer.

Red Sneaker Exercises

1) Are you hearing your lead character's voice in your head? That's a good sign. Probably. Assuming you're not hearing your own voice, improved somewhat, this probably means you have a solid understanding of who your character is and what the character might sound like. You don't have to use first-person narration to bring out that unique voice, though. You can do it in dialogue, or even internal monologue. Is there something unique about this story that will benefit from a character speaking directly to the reader?

2) In *The Catcher in the Rye*, Salinger restricts us to Holden Caulfield's voice so we are immersed in his restricted and troubled worldview. The plot is all but irrelevant. The appeal of the story is understanding who Holden is and empathizing with his alienated viewpoint. Is there a reason why readers would benefit from a restricted, possibly even unreliable viewpoint in your story?

3) The principal tradeoff in first-person narration is that although readers may feel they get a more profound understanding of the lead character—every other character will seem sketchy by comparison. At best, the reader will understand how the viewpoint character perceives others, but any more profound understanding will come, if at all, through careful reading between the lines. Will that work in your novel? Can your story survive if the reader only has one character they understand to any significant degree? Do you need to introduce other viewpoints—even if you maintain first-person narration for the main character?

REVEALING CHARACTER EMOTIONS

"Show the readers everything, tell them nothing."

— ERNEST HEMINGWAY

I still remember the moment with clarity. We were doing an author Q&A during lunch at the annual writers conference. Someone made the usual comment about how writers should "show, not tell"—and my longtime friend Kathleen Park called us on it. "People always say that," she countered from the audience. "But let's face it—sometimes you just have to tell. Otherwise, the story never goes anywhere."

And you know what? She's right.

After a long moment of thought, I grasped the discrepancy between what we were saying and what she was saying. When writers talk about "showing," they're usually referring not to plot details, but to character emotions (although the same is true of descriptions, as discussed in a later chapter). When you simply tell the reader about a character's emotions, it has little impact. "Sally was sad." So what? Barely even registers. If you want reader impact, you create a vivid mental image readers can absorb. "Sally raced up the stairs, slammed her bedroom door, threw herself on the bed and pounded the pillows, tears streaming from her eyes." Ok, over the top, but you get the idea. Create a vivid image with your words.

Here's a question to consider. Is that image better with or without the tears? To me, the tears are so obvious it's better without them. Adding tears comes perilously close to telling.

Revealing emotional states is even more challenging when you're dealing with a character with suppressed or repressed emotions, like my longtime series character Ben Kincaid. Because he tended to keep his feelings bottled up inside, I devised all sorts of indirect indicators to communicate his feelings to the reader. I think these were key to the widespread character empathy that spawned nineteen novels. As you know from *Creating Character*, letting readers feel a connection to your protagonist is necessary for immersion in the story. That's why I encourage you to think about backstory, to complete character job applications, and such. Similarly, in *Perfecting Plot*, I urged you to think about character arc, hero's journeys, and the long-form story you're telling.

How do you reveal the emotions that lie beneath the surface? As it turns out, it's much the same in fiction as in real life. You can draw from your own experiences to create three-dimensional characters who are portrayed with art and subtlety.

The first and most obvious approach is body language. We all know the body indicates emotions (far better than words). That's why we have our characters smile, shrug, breathe deeply, whisper, etc. The problem here is that a little goes a long way, it soon becomes repetitive, and some body-language indicators are so obvious that it is basically telling.

Another approach is to deliberately portray the character having an over- or underreaction. When someone suddenly flies off the handle for no apparent reason, it usually indicates something is simmering inside. Daniel Pike usually appears confident and genial, so if he suddenly erupts, or has any extreme emotion—you know something is bothering him. The same is true for an unnatural underreaction. Either way, it cues the reader that something unstated is troubling the character, and encourages them to figure out what it is. Another mystery to solve, which always keeps readers turning pages.

You don't have to be a poker player to know that **tics and tells often reveal what someone is thinking.** Everyone has a tell, they say, and so should your protagonist. The reader may not recognize the tell at first—but they will in time, and that will be a wonderful epiphanic moment that will not only let them feel smart but will also inspire them to think that you are a skilled writer. Ben Kincaid stuttered when he was worried, or was experiencing some other suppressed emotion. Sometimes he tugged at his collar. What's happening with your character? My advice: try to avoid the obvious—like averting eyes or clearing throats. Come up with something less on-the-nose, something readers may not immediately grasp, but will love when they get it and will relish when it reoccurs—because they now know what it means, without being told.

You've read about the fight-or-flight response. Which will your protagonist choose? Most heroes will fight—eventually. (This is why I never took to the Scooby Doo crew. What kind of heroes run when they see the monster?) But perhaps fighting is not your protagonist's first response. Maybe it's something they have to work up to. Will your character choke? This might give you an opening for a great character arc. The character eventually finds strength they didn't realize they possessed.

Finally, consider whether a passive-aggressive response might reveal what is swirling beneath the surface. (This might be better for a sidekick character than the main hero.) Entire books have been written about passive-aggression, but the general idea is that someone superficially acquiesces, but does so in a way that suggests hostility. If you ask your partner if they want to go to the movies and they answer, "We could do that"—is that a "yes"? "Sure, if you want to" is similarly passive-aggressive. "You do whatever you want. You always do" is edging closer to plain aggression, but it definitely reveals suppressed emotions. This is another reason to write "off-the-nose" dialogue, which as I explained in *Dynamic Dialogue*, is often the most interesting to read.

You can use some or all of these techniques if you find them useful. What is paramount is that you give the reader an opportunity to connect to your main character. When readers identify, even though the character is completely unlike them—that's when the magic happens. That's when the reader feels they're on the page, experiencing this story as it transpires, learning the lessons, without undergoing the misery you put the character through. That is the hallmark of a great book. And you can do it.

HIGHLIGHTS/EXERCISES

Highlights

1) "Show, don't tell" refers to the way you reveal characters' emotions to readers.

2) Develop tools for indicating emotions without explicitly expressing them.

3) The best emotion indicator is body language.

4) Another approach is to describe deliberate over- or underreactions.

5) Create character tics and tells to suggest a character's emotions.

6) A character's fight-or-flight response is informative.

7) A passive-aggressive response can indicate what is swirling beneath the surface.

Red Sneaker Exercises

1) Try writing a short scene with no "telling" whatsoever. No overt indications of emotional states, no adverbs after "he said," no giveaway dramatic exchanges. For an added challenge, write the description so it is also suggested rather than directly described. Can you do it? If you can bring this off, a less extreme approach, restricting "telling" to infrequent occasions, should be a snap.

2) In *Dynamic Dialogue*, I discussed the value of avoiding dialogue attributions that "tell" readers how the dialogue should be read—because the reader should get that from the way the dialogue was written. Similarly, readers should be able to understand the emotional context of a scene from how it is written. Does the reader understand the various characters' goals? Does the reader understand how the characters feel about one another? Can you make the preparation for the scene so complete that "telling" is no longer necessary?

4

WHEN DO I NEED PERMISSION?

"And by the way, everything in life is writable about if you have the outgoing guts to do it, and the imagination to improvise. The worst enemy to creativity is self-doubt."

— SYLVIA PLATH

I hear this question almost every time I host a writing retreat or WriterCon:

When do I need permission?

To write? Never. Wait around for that and you'll never publish anything.

To mention celebrities in my book? Never. But I would be careful about what you say. Why offend? You don't need a lawsuit in your life.

To mention real-life places? Never, but again, don't ask for trouble. If the description is going to be negative in some way, make it up, like my make-believe country club in *Cruel Justice*. There are country clubs in Tulsa, but since the one in my book was going to have a bad father and potential murderer on the grounds, I invented one. And just to be safe, I put it in a location where no country club could possibly be. No lawsuits. (But a few emails from folks telling me they'd been to Tulsa and couldn't find the country club.)

To mention the title of a book, song, or movie? Never. That's like referencing a fact. You aren't infringing on anything copyrighted so you don't need permission.

To include a link to something on the web? Never. It's just a link. This is true even if the link is to something that shouldn't be on the web, like work still under copyright protection. You can't upload copyrighted work, but if someone else has, you can link to it.

To quote something in the public domain? Never. If it's not protected by copyright, you can quote with wild abandon. Currently under US law, everything published before 1924 (and some work published after) is in the public domain.

To quote or reproduce someone else's creative work?

Ah, now we have a tricky question. This takes us into the realms of permission and fair use, so I'm going to get legal on you, but I hasten to say (as I am required to do) that I am not your lawyer, I do not represent you, this should in no way be taken as me offering legal advice, and you should always consult your own attorney before taking action. Understood?

I frequently see manuscripts from writers in my Patreon program that use song lyrics as an epigraph. I had one recently with dozens of song lyrics spread throughout the book (you know who you are). Generally speaking, if you want to quote more than one line of a lyric, you need to ask for permission and you will almost certainly be paying someone a licensing fee. What constitutes one line? There is no clear legal rule on that. Is it a musical phrase? A complete grammatical sentence? No one knows for sure, so again, my advice is, don't risk it. Use as little as possible, or none at all.

For one of my earliest novels, *Perfect Justice,* I wanted to use a Mary Chapin-Carpenter song lyric that I thought beautifully and meaningfully reflected the theme of the book. Just four phrases, arguably two lines. And my publisher told me they'd contacted her music publisher and this would be no problem. They'd just deduct the $800 from my royalties.

I switched to a quote from Blaise Pascal. He's long dead and thus no longer charging fees.

How much can you quote from a source? Some people still say one line, even when you're quoting prose. Some have tossed around a "300 words" rule. Some say no more than 10% of an article. But none of these rules are enshrined in law. They are guidelines, not absolutes. So the safest course is always to err on the side of quoting as little as possible.

This leads us to the doctrine of "**fair use**," one of the muddiest areas of the law. Courts have allowed critics and other nonfiction writers to quote copyrighted work, but what constitutes "fair use" is a judgment call, and getting judgments from judges is expensive and risky. The court will apply four criteria to its decision:

1) **Purpose**: Is the quote for commercial use, or not-for-profit/educational use?

2) **Nature**: Facts can't be protected, but creative work gets the strongest possible protection.

3) **Quantity**: The more you quote, the more likely you are to run into trouble. Most publishers limit quotations to 200-300 words from a single source.

4) **Market Impact**: Will your quoting deter readers from purchasing the quoted work? Have you made the source unnecessary or irrelevant?

The safest course, natch, is to not quote. But if you must and you think there's potential danger, ask your publisher, or if you don't have one, consult an intellectual property lawyer.

Remember: Identifying or citing the source does NOT mean you no longer need permission to quote.

And by the way, the same essential rules apply to visual works. Get permission, pay a fee.

HIGHLIGHTS/EXERCISES

Highlights

1) You don't need permission to mention real-life people or places—but if you plan to say derogatory things, it might be safer to fictionalize.

2) You don't need permission to mention the title of a song, film, television program, or any other work of art.

3) You don't need permission to link to anything on the web.

4) You don't need permission to quote something in the public domain, that is, no longer protected by copyright.

5) You can generally quote one line of a song lyric without paying a fee.

6) To quote more than a few words from a copyrighted work, you will need permission and may need to pay a licensing fee.

7) Though courts allow some quoting of prose works under the "fair use" doctrine, what constitutes fair use is judged on a case-by-case basis.

8) The factors courts will consider when determining what constitutes fair use are: purpose, nature, quantity, and market impact.

9) When in doubt—don't quote someone else's work without permission.

Red Sneaker Exercises

1) Before you go down the long and difficult road of obtaining permission and paying a fee, ask yourself whether the quotation is truly essential to your work. It might be fun to quote a favorite song, but is it necessary? Could you do as well with a paraphrase? Or better yet, could you write a song lyric of your own and have a fictional character quote it?

5

PROTECTING YOUR WORK

"Every secret of a writer's soul, every experience of his life, every quality of his mind, is written large in his works."

— VIRGINIA WOOLF

I'm not sure why, but there seems to be a pervasive fear among the pre-published that their creative work will be stolen before they finish writing it. "What if someone steals my idea?" or "I don't want to share my big plot twist because someone might copy it." I try to comfort students, explaining that this really doesn't happen in the book world—but they are rarely assuaged. I don't know if this is the normal anxiety of the creative, or abnormal egoism suggesting their concept is so brilliant anyone could have a bestseller if they just heard a whisper of the central idea. Let me try to set the record straight and, I hope, put some minds to rest.

You Can't Protect Ideas. Everyone knows the primary protection for written work is the copyright—but you can't copyright ideas. Only written work. Until you've written it down, there's nothing to protect (and even then, copyright only protects your arrangement of words, not the ideas underlying them). Arthur C. Clarke once famously came up with the idea of communication satellites and tried to patent it—without success. You can't patent an idea. You need an actual invention. Same thing with copyright. You can't copyright an idea. Only a piece of writing.

The Myth of Bestselling Ideas. Perhaps you think your concept is so unique anyone could make a success of it. The history of literature suggests otherwise. Granted, there is a lot of talk in New York about "high concept"—a clever juxtaposition of popular tropes, or perhaps a reversal of norms, so unique that a brief description of the premise creates interest in the book. To be sure, a good tagline can generate interest. But at the end of the day, the only thing that will make a book a success is good, immersive writing. Typically, many books can and will be written on the same general concept. The one that has the best sales is not necessarily the first one. The most successful book will be the best one. Something some other writer cobbled together in a hurry will not steal your thunder.

Bottom line—even with so-called high-concept novels, it is rarely the idea that makes the book a success. It's the quality of the writing. The best way to protect your idea will be to work hard, write every day, produce a high-quality novel employing your idea—and get it into print. So share your work with colleagues, beta readers, agents, editors—and stop worrying about it.

Do I Need a Copyright? Copyright is not necessary to protect your work. Your writing is automatically protected the moment you write it down. You obtain a formal copyright (which you can do online—*www.copyright.gov*) to create proof in the event ownership should be challenged. In other words, you're not creating a copyright, you're proving it already existed on a certain date.

Is it worth it? If it gives you peace of mind, sure. But the truth is, this will only be relevant in the extremely unlikely event that someone steals this unpublished work by an unknown writer, publishes it, and makes money off it. What are the chances of that happening?

Public Domain. Are you concerned that your work might accidentally slip into the public domain if you don't protect it? Perhaps you've read about moviemakers who lost their rights because they didn't guard them zealously. That doesn't happen to books. In our world, work is copyrighted for the life of the author PLUS seventy years—long enough to protect you and a generation or two of your heirs. The only way your work can slip into the public arena is if you purposefully choose to make it available to one and all—say, through the Creative Commons license, or some similar program by which authors deliberately make their work available and reproducible. Even if you do that, though, you still retain the copyright. It's no different from signing a contract with a publishing house. You license the right to publish the book—but you do not give away your copyright.

I think some of this insecurity arises because we live in a world where movies and tv shows get more media attention than books (which is so wrong, but don't get me started). You hear stories out of Hollywood about people stealing ideas and being sued because someone alleges they stole an idea. This happens in large part because these media projects are by nature collaborative. Many people are involved in the production of a film, including, typically, the writing of the screenplay. Over the course of multiple drafts of multiple screenplays, some ideas may be retained, but not everyone's name will appear in the final credits (much less on a check). So lawsuits happen, but they are expensive and rarely successful. Unless you're collaborating with hundreds of people on your book, you should able to avoid this problem.

What About eBook Piracy? You may have read about people who have created self-pubbed eBooks on Amazon by duplicating the work of other writers in whole or part. This sadly is happening—but it's not the idea being stolen, it's the arrangement of words. Amazon will pull a pirated book when this is brought to their attention. Most of these people are trying to make some quick money before they're caught. It's sad that people like this exist in the world, but there's nothing new about unscrupulous losers trying to rip off artists. If you've been listening to the Red Sneaker podcast (and if not, why aren't you?), you've heard me praise Nora Roberts, who has taken action against one such South American author. Roberts realizes that not every writer has the financial wherewithal to fight this fight —so she will. She's a hero in our own time.

The Importance of Exposure. It's just possible that unrestrained distribution of your work, or some of it, might be to your benefit. You're probably aware that some people are giving away eBooks, making them available for free—to generate interest in their work. Paulo Coelho says he pirates his own work to gain exposure—and it works. People like Anna Todd, the author of *After* (now a major film), made their work available free of charge on Wattpad to generate a following, and that exposure has led to six-digit contracts with established publishing houses. Andy Weir famously posted *The Martian* on his webpage, chapter by chapter, getting feedback that helped him make that book a runaway success.

Here are my Final Thoughts: I'm glad you have confidence in your ideas and your work. That's a good sign. But the best thing you can do now is stop worrying about bogeymen in the closet and focus on finishing your book. Make it the best book you can, attend a conference to learn how to survive in the book world, and get your work into print. Become the success story you want—and then you'll never have to worry about insubstantial specters again. Because you'll be too busy worrying about what to write next.

HIGHLIGHTS/EXERCISES

Highlights

1) You can't copyright, trademark, or patent an idea.

2) No one is likely to steal your idea—and even if they did, the execution would be completely different from yours.

3) What makes a book brilliant is rarely the idea—and always the way it is written.

4) Piracy occurs when an author steals another author's arrangement of words.

5) Don't worry about "idea theft" and instead focus on the writing process, prewriting, writing, revising, receiving criticism, and everything that will make your book the best it can possibly be.

Red Sneaker Exercises

1) At best, ideas are starting points. To be sure, they are nice to have, but at the end of the day, what makes a book special will be how well you write it. Instead of worrying about being robbed by unknowns desperate for someone else's ideas, think about how you can execute this idea to make the most of it. What spin can you put on this idea that no one will anticipate? How can you create a unique experience rather than another version of something people have seen many times before?

6

DESCRIPTION READERS
WON'T SKIP

"Don't tell me the moon is shining; show me the glint of light on broken glass."

—ANTON CHEKHOV

I discussed description at WriterCon in the midst of a talk titled "Five Super-Secret Steps to Superior Fiction." Obviously, I chose this title primarily due to my addiction to alliteration, but also because the elements of great session topics are, first, numbered lists, and second, the suggestion that you're revealing secrets. The problem, of course, was that having devised this brilliant title, I needed to come up with an equally brilliant list of super-secrets.

I don't know how brilliant the talk was, but I did come up with a list. And one of the super-secret steps related to description. I talked for maybe ten minutes about description, but I didn't notice the audience looking as if I'd revealed the arcane secrets of the ancients. Less is more, I said, and they nodded in agreement. One insightful sentence is better that a long-winded paragraph. Sure, Bill, what else is new? But I finally saw eyes widen when I said:

You have five senses. Use them.

What did that mean?

I have noticed two recurring patterns in my small-group writing workshops. First: when early writers start describing, they typically write about how something looks. In other words, the use only one sense—sight. This is understandable. Sight is the sense we use most often. When people think about description, they typically consider how something looks. I've even attended workshops where speakers told readers to "Imagine your scene on a television screen. Write what you see."

This is horrible advice. Limiting yourself to one sense is like typing with one finger. Why? Typically, describing appearances alone leads to the most superficial and least impactful descriptions. You're basically telling readers what they conjured in their minds' eyes the instant you said "courtroom" or "blanket" or "sunset." And if they already have a mental image of the scene, no verbal description is likely to dislodge it.

Second: early writers tend toward pleasant, lovely descriptions—lots of sunsets and wind-whipped ocean views—even when the book is a mystery or thriller. Regardless of your genre, you want your story to have tension, to give readers the unsettling feeling that all is not as it should be (as discussed in a later chapter). That's how you keep readers turning pages. You can't do that with rambling portraits of beautiful landscapes. You use skillful description to inject tension—by using all of your senses in close collaboration.

Let me take you through an example, mostly cribbed from my friend David Morrell.

He sat on the blanket.

Not a terribly exciting sentence, is it? I'll dress it up with some description.

He sat on the gray blanket.

Oh, good work, Bill. Much better. You added an adjective. You took something that should be warm and comforting—a blanket —and turned it into something dull and uninteresting—gray. Surely we can do better—without interrupting the pace of this obviously breathtaking story.

He sat on the blanket. It reeked of sweat.

Okay…this is a little better. One strong word is better than a dozen weak ones, and "reeked" is a strong word that immediately conjures a powerful mental image. You can almost smell the stink. Plus, the blanket is sweaty, which means it feels wet and icky. So now we've activated three senses—sight, touch, smell. I'm not going to make the guy taste the sweaty blanket, but we could still plus this a little…

He sat on a gray scratchy blanket that reeked of sweat.

You can decide for yourself whether you prefer two short sentences or one slightly longer one, or whether you want to put a comma between the adjectives. The choice depends upon the pace you're creating. If this is a tense, suspenseful, scary scene, go with the short sentences. A longer sentence does create a some-what more relaxed, leisurely pace.

The big addition here is the word "scratchy." This adds another unpleasant suggestion about how the blanket feels—and perhaps a sound cue as well. Scratchy blankets make noise, so the overall takeaway is irritating, off-putting. To create tension in your scene, you've inserted a blanket, something that we normally think of as comforting, but here it's just the opposite, because of a few descriptive elements. It's gray. Blah. Reeks. Ick. Sweaty. Gross. And scratchy. Something you want to get rid of, not wrap around yourself. You've only used a few words, but you've created a vivid word picture that will have far more impact on the reader than a long-winded description based solely upon sight.

A good approach to every scene—including the descriptive parts—is to remind yourself what emotional tone you're striving to achieve before you start to write it. Is this scene romantic? Suspenseful? Humorous? Heart-breaking? If you have a clear idea what you're striving for, you're far more likely to achieve it. The old woman on the park bench could evoke pathos—or joy— depending upon how the description is written. The single man with a neatly folded handkerchief could suggest loneliness—or an orderly mind. The emotions you evoke are dependent upon how well you describe it. Remember that you have five senses and use them all. In most cases, the reader can adequately supply the visual image. You supply the rest.

HIGHLIGHTS/EXERCISES

Highlights

1) Write descriptions that evoke all five senses.

2) Use the sense of sight—writing about how something looks—least, not most.

3) Use description to develop the emotional tone you want for your scene.

4) Use unexpected combinations to enrich your descriptions.

5) Less is more.

Red Sneaker Exercises

1) Try writing a scene with no visual description whatsoever. Make no reference to how anything looks. Instead, focus on the other senses. How does it feel? How does it taste ?

2) Think about the emotional tone of the scene. How can you evoke or enhance that through description? For instance, the sense of smell is said to be the one most closely linked to memory. If you're trying to create a mood of nostalgia, or déjà vu, maybe you should add some olfactory enhancement. What mood—and corresponding description—is right for the scene you're writing?

3) Try writing a descriptive passage without using the word "was." This may be challenging, especially if you tend to rely upon visual description. Sentences using "to-be" verbs will never be the best (see *Sizzling Style*), but a long passage of "was" sentences will be the most static, unengaging description imaginable. Train yourself to do without it. The further you get from visual description, the easier this will be.

7

REVISING YOUR WAY TO EXCELLENCE

"When your story is ready for rewrite, cut it to the bone. Get rid of every ounce of excess fat. This is going to hurt; revising a story down to the bare essentials is always a little like murdering children, but it must be done."

— STEPHEN KING

Just to be clear, this essay isn't about editing. Just as well, since I've already written an entire book on that subject (*Excellent Editing*). That book discussed the entire writing process, though, and this piece is specifically about revision—revision for writers, revision designed not just to eliminate typos but to turn an okay manuscript into a superb one.

"Every writer has their own way of doing things," Patrick Rothfuss says, and he's probably right about that. But I also think there are some essential steps when revising your manuscript, and you cannot skip any of them without undermining the quality of your work. So you finish your first draft—an impressive accomplishment. Once you've got a first draft, the chances that you will finish this book increase dramatically, and of course, if you finish, the chances that you'll publish increase dramatically. So let's revise this book to improve your chances of finishing, publishing, and breaking out big time, attracting the readers you need to make writing not just an avocation, but a vocation. Something you can do profitably for the rest of your life.

Six (Maybe Seven) Steps to the Revision Process
1) The Developmental Review

Some people call this the developmental edit, but that always traumatizes me, because "edit" suggests making changes to the words, and there's no point in doing that at this stage because so much is going to change. The idea is to get some useful outside input before you've spent so much time on it that everything is etched in stone. This is very much revision—it's simply revision that may take place before you complete a draft.

My former editor Joe Blades was a wonderful man who read everything I wrote and made genuinely valuable editorial suggestions—a concept that seems quaintly archaic in this modern era when "editors" are in meetings all day and rarely edit. For my last book at Ballantine, long after Joe departed, after getting no feedback for months, I finally asked my young editor if she was planning to edit the book. "Oh, did you want me to?" Yes, the publishing world has changed.

You may need to phone a friend or hire someone for this, but it's worth doing, because the truth is no author sees everything. Joe offered comments based upon my outline. You probably want to have some pages down, maybe a first draft, or at the least a completed first act. This is the time for someone to point out problems like—your protagonist is not interesting or likeable, the plot takes too long to get started, there's no tension, no conflict, you have long boring parts or excessive description, etc. I offer developmental critiques when asked and time permits, and I prefer to have a complete first draft (among other reasons, because the climax is so important), but I don't insist upon it. You just need to have written enough that the reviewer can make intelligent contributions that save you time—by spotting something early so you don't write several flawed drafts.

2) Self-Revision

No developmental edit is going to take the place of the author working over their own manuscript carefully. I've written many novels, but I've never let one of them out the door in fewer than ten drafts, and I think that's one reason my books have developed a positive reputation. Some people can do it in fewer drafts (people who aren't psycho perfectionists), but I can't imagine a good book being achieved in fewer than five drafts. For me, the first draft is the painful process of getting all the words down. The second and perhaps third drafts are about solidifying the plot, which despite my outlining still largely emerges during the writing. Thrillers require airtight plots, so I take my time and try to get it right. At least one draft focuses on the characters. The most important is the protagonist, but all the main characters are important, all need to be distinct and memorable, all need to speak and behave differently. The last several drafts should focus on the language. Go over it slowly, read it backwards—whatever works for you.

3) Alpha/Beta Readers

People use these terms differently. To me, the author is the alpha reader, so I send my manuscripts out to beta readers. Some people say the writer is not a reader, due to the complete impossibility of seeing your own work objectively. Some people send the first wave out to other writers, to catch technical problems only writers would catch, and then to readers, who can say whether it's good, interesting, or any fun. I do both at once—targeting people who write, but are not so far removed from the pleasures of reading that they can't enjoy a book as a reader too.

How many do you need? I don't know, how many have you got? At WriterCon one year Phillip Margolin said that he has ten beta readers. His theory was that if only one raises a particular objection, it's an outlier, safely ignored, but if six people say the same thing, it's time to revise. My insecurities are sufficient that one complaint would be sufficient to inspire me to take another look. I think every criticism should be considered, but at the end of the day, it's your book, and you have to make sure it is what you want it to be. Just don't reject anything out of hand. You're only cheating yourself. The point of having beta readers is not to have a cheering squad telling you how wonderful you are. The point is to help you see what you haven't seen yet.

4) The Line Edit

Everyone needs a good line edit, and no, the line editor cannot be the writer. You're too close. You won't see the problems. Trust me, this is something worth paying for. You don't want to be among the hordes of writers uploading books riddled with problems that draw readers out of the story, erode confidence, and cause mortification. Get someone who will carefully go over the manuscript line by line. Anything that improves the pace, rhythm, or readability of your book is a plus. I regularly do these edits for people I know. Friends don't let friends publish bad books.

5) Read It Aloud

I used to scoff at the concept of reading books aloud during the revision process, and I still don't think it's a good way to judge the substantive content. When authors read aloud, they start adding inflection, drama, pace variation, and other cues that the non-author reader will not have. You should be trying to duplicate the reader experience, not practicing for your future book reading.

But I have learned to appreciate the value of reading a book aloud as part of the line-editing process. I've read the audiobook for my nonfiction books, but only with the Daniel Pike series did I start reading the audiobooks for novels. What an eyeopener! The first time I did it, I could barely finish a page without encountering some flawed line of Bill-prose I couldn't wait to revise. By the second time I recorded a novel, I took my laptop into the recording room with me so I could make changes as I encountered them before I forgot them. Let me tell you—this not only improved the book but allowed me to catch many potentially embarrassing errors.

Does this mean the prior line edit was inadequate? No. No one catches everything. Even books from big New York publishers contain mistakes in the first edition. This is often how collectors can distinguish a first edition from later editions. No book is perfect. But since you're reading the book aloud anyway, why not edit as you go and make the book even better than it already is?

6) The Gift of Time

If you drive too close to the deadline, you lose the luxury of putting a manuscript away for a while, getting it out of your head, then re-experiencing it as a reader rather than the author. This can make a huge difference. When you're writing, you miss things because you're too close. But time can erode that disability. For various complex publishing reasons, *The Game Master* sat on the shelf for two years between when I thought it was finished and when it was actually going to be available. When I pulled up that manuscript after being away from it for two years—I was horrified. Who wrote this mess? How did I miss these glaring problems? Needless to say, the book was improved as a result, and now whenever possible I give myself the luxury of putting a book away for a time, then re-reading it before I send it off to be published.

7) Formatting

One last note for those who self-publish. Formatting is almost as important as line editing. If a book looks unprofessional, it has the same negative impact as a book riddled with typos. It puts off readers. It allows them to get judgy and cast scorn on your work for reasons that have nothing to do with the content. If you use a Mac, get Vellum. It's a great program and well worth the financial investment. Vellum also deals with the fact that we have no universal standard for eBooks. Vellum will give you a separate file for Kindle, Kobo, rtf, print, etc. You will have to learn how to use it but it's an intuitive program and you'll pick it up quickly. If you're on a PC, Scrivener may be your best option (but if I were you, I would go to the mall and get a Mac. Seriously. You're a writer. You need the best.) You have the technological means to make your book look as good as the ones coming from large publishers. So do it.

Bottom line: You've put a lot of work into this manuscript. Don't quit before the job is done. Revise your way to success.

HIGHLIGHTS/EXERCISES

Highlights

1) Revision is critical to your success as a writer.

2) Consider getting developmental input on your work early in the process, after the first draft if not earlier.

3) Learn to be your own best editor—but not your only editor.

4) Use beta readers, outside independent eyes that can see problems you can't.

5) Make sure your work gets a thorough line edit before you publish.

6) Consider reading the work aloud—possibly as you record the audiobook—as a way of catching elusive errors.

7) When possible, put the manuscript away for a time, then pick it up again later when you can read it with fresh eyes.

8) If you plan to self-publish, make sure the interior is thoroughly vetted and formatted so that it is a pleasure to read.

Red Sneaker Exercises

1) When is it time to get outside input? When do you think you've written enough that someone can get a reasonable sense of what you're writing? Generally speaking, you should first write at least one hundred pages, but you may want to wait longer. Don't wait until you've written so many drafts you're reluctant to change anything. Ask yourself: what's right for me? When will I be most receptive to suggestions that might target problems early and prevent me from wasting time?

2) Be friendly when you attend writing workshops, retreats, or conferences. Don't be shy. Remember, in all likelihood, most of the people there are just as introverted as you are. Why do you think they spend so much time with books? But this is your opportunity to make friends and colleagues you retain for your entire professional career. It's not uncommon for writers to serve as one another's beta readers. Who would you most like to have providing input? How are you going to get them?

3) No book ever benefitted from rush. When you make your writing schedule, assume everything will take longer than you anticipate. It probably will, even if you maintain a daily writing schedule (and it will dramatically if you don't). Give yourself enough time to revise and revise, and also to set it aside for a time after you think it's finished. If you have a traditional publisher, you may be given a deadline. Start early. The deadline is not your excuse for turning in half-baked work. If you self-publish, you may create your own deadlines, telling readers when they can expect your next work. Sooner is better, but you should still pick a deadline you can make without compromising the

story. What deadline will work best for you? What deadline can you realistically meet?

4) Commit to a daily writing habit. Sign the Writer's Contract in the Appendix. Write every day till the work is done. Even if you tend to be a perfectionist or a major reviser, a daily writing habit will be the key factor in determining whether you finish that book.

5) Look at the Writer's Schedule in the Appendix. It takes into account not only the first draft but several revisions. Can you stay on track? Commit to this schedule and stick to it.

THE BLASTED BOOK DESCRIPTION

"It's not what you sell that matters as much as how you sell it!"

— BRIAN HALLIGAN

Ever tried to describe your own book? Chances are you have, and chances are you found it a difficult and unpleasant experience. If you're taking the traditional publishing route, you must write a query letter or prepare an elevator pitch. If you're self-publishing, you must write your book blurb or back cover copy. And either way—it's hard. You'd think it would be simple to describe something you've been working on for months—but it isn't.

This is why there's now a growing industry of pros who will write your book description for you. Just as you can hire out the editing or the cover design, you can get someone to write book blurbs. And if you can afford it, this is not a bad idea. We tend to get too close to our own work. Sometimes ego gets in the way. It can be useful to have an objective third party who didn't write the book, doesn't have any darlings, and is simply making an objective attempt to get readers interested in reading and buying the book.

Here are a few guidelines to follow if you decide to write your own description:

Employ strategic formatting. Remember that the visual appearance of words is an important influence on reading. Remember that most people don't actually *read* webpages (like the ones on Amazon)—they *scan* them. Long paragraphs and big blocks of text get ignored. Short paragraphs look friendlier. Visual tricks—boldface, italics, bullet points—if not used excessively, can make your text more visually appealing and can make key words stand out.

Here's a useful list that might help you get started on your book description and prevent you from leaving out anything important:

Headline-Open with a hook, something short and intriguing that immediately captures the reader's interest.

Hero-Identify the sympathetic or empathetic lead character you want the reader to cheer for.

Opponent-Identify who or what prevents your hero from obtaining their goal.

McGuffin-What is it your hero (and possibly others) want? What is the goal or desire that motivates the key players?

Stakes-What happens if the hero does not succeed, or the opponent gets their way? As you may know from reading *Powerful Premise*, stories are more compelling when the stakes are high.

Social Proof-Provide sales figures, quotes from other authors, reviews, list rankings, or similar successful titles.

Call to Action-Tell the reader what to do. The best one is "Click here." If the reader is already on your Amazon page, this may not be necessary. They probably know what to do.

And hey—was this list easier to read (or scan) because I made a list employing short graphs and boldface? Of course it was.

If you're posting on Amazon, you may need to use "coding enhancers" to make the description turn out right. You can find these at Amazon Author Central. For instance, to indicate bold-face text, you insert: <b>

Remember that you are not writing this for yourself. The point is not to gratify your literary inclinations. The point is to sell books. You should always be answering the reader's question: What's in this for me? In nonfiction, the answer will be topics of interest or potential benefit. In fiction, it will be tapping plots, tropes, and character archetypes that appeal to the reader. What's on your reader's Id List? (If you're not sure what I mean by this, listen to Red Sneaker Writers podcast #8 with psychologist Jennifer Lynn Barnes.) What will trigger readers' interest and inspire them to give your book a chance?

Ok, let's test the system. This is the book description for my novel *The Game Master*—and I chose that one because it sold more eBooks in the first three months than anything I've ever written. Here's the description:

IT'S NOT WHETHER YOU LIVE OR DIE, IT'S HOW YOU PLAY THE GAME.

WHILE IN VEGAS FOR THE AMERICAN POKER GRAND SLAM, BB Thomas—the Game Master—is suddenly arrested by the FBI and taken to a top-secret laboratory. A scientist has been murdered in a bizarre manner, and BB's daughter has been kidnapped. Reluctantly joining forces with his ex-wife, Linden, BB plunges into a labyrinthine mystery incorporating the world's oldest and best-known games and taking them to Paris, Dubai, Pyongyang, and Alexandria. Pursued by a relentless FBI agent and an unknown assailant who wants him stopped at any cost, BB races to uncover an insidious plot involving secret societies, ancient cover-ups, and savage vengeance. Someone is playing a deadly game, and the

object is the destruction of every government on the face of the earth—no matter how many people die in the process.
William Bernhardt is the bestselling author of...
Now I'll annotate the sections:

(HEADLINE) *IT'S NOT WHETHER YOU LIVE OR DIE, IT'S HOW YOU PLAY the game.*

WHILE IN VEGAS FOR THE AMERICAN POKER GRAND SLAM, **(HERO)** BB Thomas—the Game Master—is suddenly arrested by the FBI and taken to a top-secret laboratory. A scientist has been murdered in a bizarre manner, and **(McGuffin)** BB's daughter has been kidnapped. Reluctantly joining forces with his ex-wife, Linden, BB plunges into a labyrinthine mystery incorporating the world's oldest and best-known games and taking them to Paris, Dubai, Pyongyang, and Alexandria. Pursued by **(Opponents)** a relentless FBI agent and an unknown assailant who wants him stopped at any cost, BB races to uncover an insidious plot involving secret societies, ancient cover-ups, and savage vengeance. Someone is playing a deadly game, and **(Stakes)** the object is the destruction of every government on the face of the earth—no matter how many people die in the process.
(Social Proof) William Bernhardt is the bestselling author of...

The Call to Action, of course, was implicitly urging readers to click the adjoining Buy button.

See how easy it is? You can do this—in about twenty drafts. And after you think you've got it, take a few days then come back to revisit it. You'll probably find ways to improve it. Done well, this can drastically improve your book sales.

Remember that your book descriptions are searchable, so use keywords—which are actually phrases or strings of words, not individual words. "Renegade lawyer defending the innocent" is an example of a strong searchable keyword chain I've used. Insert a deliberately calculated phrase into your description that may arise in whole or part in reader searches and you will boost your visibility. Even for people simply reading the description, you will increase the appeal of the book by zeroing in on a trope or subgenre of interest. You want words that make the reader think, "Brilliant! This is exactly what I've been wanting to read." But don't overdo it. Too many of these and your description will become incoherent.

If you self-publish, you can update your description any time you like—and you should. You get a great review—add it to the top or bottom of your description. Win an award? Ditto. Your other marketing efforts, like Amazon Ads, might reveal that some phrases or keyword chains are more productive than others. This is yet another advantage of self-publishing. You can change them any time you like, without interrupting sales.

Here are a couple more examples that might help spark some ideas. When I took my first stab at writing the description for the third Daniel Pike novel, *Trial by Blood*, I wrote the typical plot summary. Meh. At least I had the sense to know it was boring. After I consulted some experts, I got this:

A billion-dollar inheritance.

A suspicious reappearance.

Can Dan dig up the secrets of the past before he's buried six feet under?

Attorney Daniel Pike's flashy courtroom antics have earned him plenty of enemies—but also freed many innocent people. When he learns that the same crooked cop who got his father locked up for life is testifying in a contested-identity suit, Dan takes the case. But it won't be easy to prove his client is the long-lost heir to an immense estate since the young man can't remember the last fourteen years...

His civil litigation becomes a criminal trial when another heir is violently murdered and the mysterious amnesiac looks like the prime suspect. Battling vanishing evidence, political interference, and a brutal attack on his life, the savvy lawyer knows he'll need to put on his best performance yet.

Can Daniel save his client's name and inheritance? Or will they both pay with their lives?

Trial by Blood is the third book in the nail-biting Daniel Pike legal thriller series. If you like sinister conspiracies, brash attorneys, and dark-alley danger, then you'll love William Bernhardt's page-turning novel.

DID YOU SEE THE KEYWORD CHAINS? DID YOU NOTICE THE SHORT sentences, short paragraphs, straight-to-the punch approach? Honestly, this isn't a great plot summary—but it's an awesome book description.

Here's a famous example, from *The Martian* by Andrew Weir. You probably know the story. Guy left behind on Mars, has to survive till the cavalry arrives to save him. Here's how I would probably write the book description: "An astronaut is stranded on Mars with no way home. He must use his skills as a botanist to survive in the brutal Martian wilderness until NASA figures out how..." Blah, blah, blah. Boring. Here's how it was handled by the writer who helped make the book a bestseller:

I'm stranded on Mars.

I have no way to communicate with Earth.

I'm in a Habitat designed to last 31 days.

If the Oxygenator breaks down, I'll suffocate. If the Water Reclaimer breaks down, I'll die of thirst. If the Hab breaches, I'll just kind of explode. If none of those things happen, I'll eventually run out of food and starve to death.

So yeah. I'm screwed.

. . .

YOU SEE THE DIFFERENCE? HOOK. SHORT GRAPHS. PERSONALITY. Attitude. High concept. And not a wasted word. Reading the description makes me want to read the book again.

Of course, if you expect great sales, you still have to write a great book. But you don't want your masterpiece to languish in obscurity, so write a description that will bring the readers you deserve.

HIGHLIGHTS/EXERCISES

Highlights

1) A good book description is key to selling books in online marketplaces—where the vast majority of books are sold today.

2) Employ strategic formatting.

3) Remember the key elements of a good book description: the hook, the hero, the opponent, the McGuffin, the stakes, the social proof, and the call to action.

4) Use keyword chains to enhance the searchability of your description.

5) Update your description when you have a good reason.

6) The best description in the world won't sell a poorly written book.

Red Sneaker Exercises

1) What's your favorite book, past or present? Try writing a good book description for it. How would you sell it online? Can you devise a good hook? What's the social proof? How much (or how little) of the story do readers need to know to be interested? Can you convey the main appeal, the high concept, without getting buried in a morass of words?

2) Now try writing a book description for your work-in-progress. After you're finished, show it to a reading friend without telling them you wrote it or that it's about the book you're writing. Would they buy the book based on this description? If not, how could you tweak it to make it more appealing?

9

THE ESSENSE OF TRUE SUSPENSE

"Suspense is worse than disappointment."

— ROBERT BURNS

If you've read *Perfecting Plot*, or for that matter, any of the other books in the Red Sneaker Writers series, you understand the importance of creating suspense, or its junior partner, tension. It's a matter of maintaining interest, keeping the reader riveted to the page in a world rife with distractions. Suspense is not just for so-called suspense novels–it's an important element in any story you want the reader to finish. And in my opinion, it's just as important in nonfiction as it is in fiction. When a book is full of suspense, the reader finishes and runs to work the next day (or posts on Amazon) enthusiastically talking about this great book everyone needs to read. That's when they call it "a good read" or say they stayed up till three in the morning because they couldn't put it down. And that is the best publicity a writer can get.

Simply stated, suspense is apprehension–the reader wondering and even worrying about what will happen on the next page. This requires at least two elements. First, there must be a perilous situation fraught with risk. This doesn't have to involve guns, cliffs, or end-of-the-world scenarios. Sometimes emotional stakes can be just as important.

The second essential element is a protagonist readers care about. This doesn't mean they have to be perfect (and they probably shouldn't be). It just means the reader has to care what happens to them. This won't happen automatically. You have to give readers a reason to care (see *Creating Character*).

Tension is nascent suspense, a sense that all is not right with the world, even if you don't know quite what the problem is. There should be tension on every page, from the first page until the climax is completed. You heard me right. **Every page.** Tension is that nagging feeling that there's a ticking time bomb somewhere that's going to explode if someone doesn't do something. It's the unsettling intimation that the characters are all talking but not actually talking about what is uppermost in their minds. Even in the early pages of the book, when you might not have fully developed the plot elements, there should be tension.

I've been reading a lot of manuscripts lately, editing for friends and patrons, and I've noticed that suspense, or attempts to create suspense, tend to fall into one of two different categories. The best kind of suspense is what I described before, a genuine concern about what might befall characters you care about. "Oh no—what will happen next?" This is conflict that arises naturally and authentically from the narrative you've created.

Too often, what I see is "false suspense." (If someone has a cooler name for this, please share it.) This is the literary equivalent of the "jump scare" in a horror film—when something unexpectedly leaps out from off-screen, usually accompanied by a deafening noise. Sure, you jump, but that scare wasn't really earned. Similarly, writers sometimes create unearned suspense by withholding vital information. In the worst possible (and most common) example, it's the fact that this exciting interlude is only a dream. Almost as bad is when a first-person narrator withholds critical information. Though some writers have done this with success (Agatha Christie, Harlan Coben), it always leaves me feeling unsatisfied. I mean, seriously–I've been inside this character's head for four hundred pages, but he never once thought about this critical detail unrevealed until the last page? To me, that's a cheat.

I understand the desire to have one last surprise on the final page, and that may be the easiest way to do it. But for me, I'd rather see a "big reveal" in the climax, and let those few pages following wrap up character business, or complete the narrative with a touching, evocative, or thematic grace note. Even in thrillers, there's more to a good novel than eternal twists and turns. And I think there should a constitutional amendment banning all dream sequences, drug trips, daydreams, parallel universes, and any other devices that allow writers to suggest something exciting is happening when it isn't. This is suspense without consequences, and I think it leaves most readers feeling swindled.

The best approach? Dynamic, sympathetic characters working against major opposition to achieve meaningful goals. Anytime you feel the suspense may be lagging–raise the stakes. Put more at risk. Put someone else in jeopardy. Make your book impossible to put down.

HIGHLIGHTS/EXERCISES

Highlights

1) Suspense is necessary for all novels.

2) Suspense is about keeping the reader riveted to the page.

3) Suspense is apprehension—making the reader worry about what might happen next.

4) Suspense requires a perilous situation.

5) Suspense requires a protagonist readers care about.

6) Tension is nascent suspense—the feeling that all is not right in the world, or that something bad is coming.

7) Avoid false suspense—tension generated by scenes that aren't real, like dreams or hallucinations.

8) Don't let your first-person narrator withhold relevant information from the reader just to generate false suspense.

9) Don't save your biggest surprise for the last page.

10) If you feel the suspense lagging—raise the stakes.

Red Sneaker Exercises

1) What scares you most? How can you get some of that on the page? Can your protagonist share your fears?

2) While readers may feel cheated if a first-person narrator knows something but doesn't reveal it, authors do not need to reveal everything they know about characters or their situation the first instant they walk on stage. Early writers have a tendency to write major infodumps into the first chapter. They know the character's backstory so they want to reveal it. But there's nothing wrong with letting the reader wait a while for the explanations. Look at your outline and character descriptions. What are the biggest reveals? How can you trickle-release them to keep the reader hooked throughout the book?

10

SHOULD YOU ATTEND A WRITER'S CONFERENCE?

"Writing is...a profession for introverts who want to tell you a story but don't want to make eye contact while doing it."

— JOHN GREEN

People often ask why I spend so much time putting together an annual writing conference. It takes time away from my writing, it's not particularly profitable, and I spend most of the year worrying that no one will come–so why? I'll explain this the same way I do everything.

Let me tell you a story.

When I was young, my dream was to write a book and see it published. That was it. That was all I wanted. I dreamed about visiting the library and seeing my name on the spine of a novel and thinking, Yeah, *I did that.* Problem was, I had no idea how to make this happen. I sent my stuff out, hundreds of times, but it was always rejected (because it was awful). I took some classes in college, but they didn't lead anywhere. I became a full-time trial lawyer, but I wrote every spare minute–and still couldn't even get an agent.

I joined a local writing group, and someone there recommended that I attend the Golden Triangle Conference in Beaumont, Texas. Not in Dallas, or Houston, or anyplace you might expect. Beaumont. Great conference, she said. So I went.

I participated in everything possible. I went to every class I could. Despite my poor social skills, I forced myself to talk to people, even agents. I even went to the banquets. No luck. But somewhere in the midst of it all, someone mentioned an agent named Esther Perkins. How did she know Esther? Esther had attended this conference several times in the past.

So after I got home, I sent Esther my manuscript (this was *Primary Justice*, in case you're wondering). She liked it. Better yet, Esther knew an editor in the Ballantine division of Random House, Joe Blades. How did she know Joe? She met him a few years before at the same conference. As it turned out, Joe also liked my book. He offered me a three-book contract. The first book was a hit and that led to a career of fifty books so far and several *New York Times* bestsellers. All because of a conference.

You may be thinking this is just my way of persuading you to attend WriterCon. Wrong. This is my explanation of why I've hosted conferences all these years.

Because now my dream is to see what happened for me, happen for you.

Can I guarantee you'll get an agent at this conference? No–though many have. Can I guarantee this will lead to a publishing contract? No, though for many it has. But I can guarantee you'll meet some terrific people, and one of them might just drop your "Esther Perkins," that is, the tiny bit of information that makes all the difference.

You'll have one asset I didn't have all those years ago–me. I'll be there chatting and shepherding and making sure everyone gets what they need. No one will miss a session that could change their life. No one will miss a chance to speak to the people they came to see. Everyone will leave feeling they have the inside scoop on the current publishing world.

Writing is like any of the arts–it's hard to know when success will strike. But the one thing I know for certain is that you have to get yourself out there, get in line, give yourself an opportunity. Your break will come when you have the right book in the right place at the right time–and you know how to take advantage of it. There is no reason why it couldn't happen for you. Do you think that skinny geeky kid from Oklahoma thirty-odd years ago had anything you don't? I did not. But I had a lot of desire. And I went to a conference.

HIGHLIGHTS/EXERCISES

Highlights

1) Attend a good writer's conference whenever possible.

Red Sneaker Exercises

1) Visit www.writercon.org and see if you can make it to WriterCon this year. I guarantee you'll be glad you did.

WHAT WRITERS NEED TO KNOW

"I think all writing is a disease. You can't stop it."

— WILLIAM CARLOS WILLIAMS

You may know some or all of this already. But these are essential bits of knowledge that, based upon my conference and retreat experiences, not everyone knows yet. So just in case...here goes.

1) The Internet Has Changed How People Find Authors

This should surprise no one. Let's face it—the near-universal availability of broadband has changed how we do everything we do. Bookstores are far from the only businesses that have suffered. You've seen the malls closing. Home delivery has become the growth area. Brick-and-mortar seems increasingly dated and largely limited to niches like groceries and clothing that seem (for now) to require in-person shopping. This has allowed Amazon to become the largest retailer in the country and the seller of over 50% of all books. If your book isn't on sale at Amazon—you have no realistic chance of developing a readership.

2) Most People Read Digitally

I know—you love the feel of a book in your hands, or the smell of a book, or the crackle of the pages, or whatever. But the truth is, most people read digitally, at least some of the time. What startles me is how many people read on their phones. I suppose the compensation for the tiny text is that your phone is always with you. When you're unexpectedly trapped in line, stuck in traffic, waiting for service, etc., you can always pull out your phone. Although dedicated eReaders are seeing diminished sales, tablets that allow you to read, and do a million other things, are quite popular. If your book doesn't have an eBook edition, you're cutting yourself off from the primary marketplace.

3) Audiobooks May Overtake Print and eBook Sales

Audiobook sales have surged in recent years. Though still considered a minority field in the book world, if this trend continues (and I think it will), audio will outpace print and perhaps even eBook sales. The ease of digital downloads, the fact that everyone carries a phone, the convenience of wireless headphones, all make this upsurge likely to continue. So if you don't have an audio edition of your book—and you can do this on your own—you're leaving money and readers on the table.

4) Self-Publishing Works

There will always be snobs out there suggesting that if you're not published by a large multinational corporation you're not as good, but the reality is, self-publishing and hybrid publishing have become the most lucrative paths for today's writers. I'm not saying there are no advantages to having a Big Five publisher, but those are diminished with the decreased role of print and bookstores. The larger profit margins available with smaller presses or self-publishing make it possible—if not commonplace—for writers to reach readers directly and make a decent income.

5) Barnes & Noble May Actually Survive

I have been cynically predicting the demise of B&N for years —and it may still happen—but being acquired by a hedge fund and installing a CEO with a good track record is the best thing to happen to our last remaining national bookstore chain in years. I remember when people decried chain stores for running independents out of business. Now they decry Amazon for running chains out of business. Whatever. If you like browsing in a physical bookstore—or seeing your books on shelves in physical bookstores—cross your fingers. B&N may yet endure.

6) Amazon Dominates

Whether B&N survives, whether the Big Five become the Big Four, whether print survives—one thing will remain true. Amazon will dominate. Amazon sells more than 50% of all books sold in the US, and in many departments (like popular fiction) the percentage is higher. The AAP or *NYT* articles suggesting that eBook sales are declining do not include Amazon sales. It seems foolish to make statements about what's selling without taking into account the by-far largest bookseller, but they do. What's amazing is that, although Amazon is America's number-one retailer, that isn't even its main business. Amazon makes more money from its cloud-computing operation, and it's also become the #3 advertising platform in the US. Don't trash Amazon, authors—you would just be shooting yourself in the foot.

7) Amazon Publishing May Be the Most Desirable Traditional Publisher

Just to be clear, I'm not talking about self-publishing your work through Kindle Direct Publishing. I'm talking about Amazon's publishing branch, which is a traditional publisher with a fabulous sales record. Are there advantages to having a publisher with a direct connection to America's greatest retailer? Obviously. If you didn't believe it before, say when Patricia Cornwell signed with them, surely you were convinced when Dean Koontz signed a multi-book deal with them. Koontz could publish anywhere he wanted, but he chose Amazon Publishing. Its "no-middleman" approach allows it to pay royalties at a rate no one else can match. If you want a traditional publisher, this one should be at the top of your list.

8) Every Writer Must Market

Once upon a time, marketing was left to specialists and writers were encouraged to stay out of it. That was largely because publishers didn't want them asking awkward questions like, Why did you spend a 100K on this author's campaign and nothing on mine? Today, everyone direct-markets. Writers must be active on social media, develop email lists, take out ads, etc. Even traditional publishers are building and maintaining email lists, possibly the most valuable commodity in the marketing world today.

9) Your Competition Is Not Other Authors

I think the writing community is the most generous bunch of people in the world. I rarely sense envy or competitiveness among authors and that's as it should be, because now more than ever, your competition is not the other writer in your genre. Your competition is Netflix and YouTube and video games. Those consume fantastic amounts of people's free time. Repeatedly, I've heard people say they have no time to read anymore—and a moment later they're chatting about a tv series they binge-watched in a day. YouTube videos have almost eradicated how-to books. Wikipedia has eliminated many reference books that sold steadily for decades. What we all need to do—together—is convince people to rediscover the more immersive and lasting benefits of a book.

10) Books Are Not Dead

I bet I don't need to convince you, right? And yet, you still hear people say this, or read articles suggesting it. It's nonsense. The forms have evolved, but people haven't stopped reading. Earlier this year, a *NYT* article quoted with dismay Pew Research Center data indicating that 24% of Americans didn't read a book in 2017. Guess what? That means that 76% of all Americans *did* read a book. How can you say something is dying when 3/4ths of the population is doing it? I consider audiobooks reading—and they've surged in popularity. Poetry is more popular than it has been in decades—though that popularity is mostly coming from Instagram, not the English Department. eBook clubs like Kindle Unlimited are allowing many to read more books than ever before. Print may ultimately become rare, but reading will never die.

So you keep writing. Keep pursuing your dream. You've got a story to tell. And the world is waiting to hear it.

HIGHLIGHTS/EXERCISES

Highlights

1) Today, most readers discover authors and buy books online.

2) Most readers read digitally—and soon everyone will, at least part of the time.

3) Audiobooks have surged in popularity and will continue to do so in the future.

4) Self-publishing is a viable alternative for writers.

5) Amazon dominates book sales.

6) Amazon Publishing may be the most desirable traditional publisher.

7) Writers must participate in marketing if they want their books to sell.

8) Your competition is not other writers—it's non-reading time-suckers like television and the internet and video games.

9) Reading is not dead—and never will be.

10) You've got a story to tell. And the world is waiting to hear it. So keep writing.

Red Sneaker Exercises

1) Ask yourself this: If you could write and publish any kind of book—what would it be? If you could have any publisher you wanted, who would it be? If you could win any imaginable writing award, what would it be? Okay, now you know your goal. Map out a plan to get there. Start by acquiring knowledge. Read good books and attend writers conferences. Next, focus on your writing. Write every day, and take your manuscript to workshops and retreats. Then follow your chosen plan to publication. Don't expect it to happen overnight. It won't. But if you are persistent —it can happen for you.

APPENDIX A: THE WRITER'S CONTRACT

Commit to getting the job done. Sign this contract. Get the rest of the family to sign as witnesses.

I, _____, hereinafter known as "the Writer," in consideration of these premises, hereby agree as follows:

1. Because I have something to say and I want readers to hear it, the aforementioned Writer will undertake a long-term, intensive writing project. The Writer agrees to work ___ hours a day, regardless of external distractions or personal circumstances. The Writer agrees to maintain this schedule until the writing project is completed.

2. The Writer understands that this is a difficult task and that there will be days when he/she does not feel like writing or when others make demands upon the Writer's writing time. The Writer will not allow this to interfere with the completion of the agreement made in paragraph one (1) of this contract.

3. The Writer also understands that good physical and mental

health is essential to the completion of any writing project. Therefore, in order to complete the agreement made in paragraph one (1), the Writer commits to a serious program of self-care, which shall include but shall not be limited to: adequate sleep, healthy diet, exercise, the relinquishment of bad habits, and reading time.

_____

Signature of the Writer and Witnesses

APPENDIX B: THE WRITER'S CALENDAR

Is it possible to finish a top-quality manuscript in six months? Of course it is, if you're willing to do the work necessary to make it happen. Here's how you do it.

Week 1

Commit to your writing schedule.

Find your writing place.

Inform friends and family that you are undertaking a major project and you would like their support.

Consider what you want to write. Start thinking like a writer.

Week 2

Commit to a premise—then make it bigger. Is it big and unique enough to attract a publisher?

Commit to a genre. What's your spin on the genre? How will you make it the same—but different? Research as needed.

Week 3

Develop your main protagonist and antagonist.

What are their best qualities—and worst? What drives them?

What is your protagonist's character arc? What does he/she want, seek, desire?

Write a half-page example of dialogue for each major character in their distinct voice.

Week 4

Put all major events (scenes) on index cards, approximately sixty total.

Arrange cards by acts. Highlight the Plot Turning Points and Character Turning Points.

Type the index cards into an outline, adding detail when you have it.

Week 5

Think about the shape of your story—the Plot. Will your character experience positive growth or maturation? Redemption? Disillusionment?

Map out twists and turns to maintain reader interest. What is the last twist the reader will suspect?

Don't shy away from a great scene because it doesn't fit your story as you currently understand it. See if you can change the story to accommodate the great scene.

Weeks 6-18

Write at least five pages every day—ten on Saturdays. No editing. Just keep moving ahead.

Do additional writing as necessary to complete 10 % of the book each week.

Week 19-23

Perform triage on what you've written. Revise. Then revise more. Focus on character consistency, character depth. Are the characters sympathetic or empathetic?

Focus on plot, pacing, story logic, theme. Is the story plausible?

Week 24-26
Give the manuscript to trusted reader(s).

Obtain comments from readers. Incorporate comments from readers where appropriate.

Set it aside for a time, then reread it with fresh eyes. Do you see problems you didn't spot before?

And then—
Attend writing conferences and bounce your ideas off agents and editors. If people don't ask to see your manuscript, your premise needs work. If people ask to see pages but don't take you on, it suggests your manuscript is not yet ready. Consider attending a small-group writing retreat to give your book that final push it needs to be publishable.

APPENDIX C: TERMS WRITERS NEED TO KNOW

The writing world has undergone tremendous changes since the so-called digital revolution of 2009. Ebooks and audiobooks have surged, small presses and self-publishing have become viable, and the online marketplace has become the dominant arena where books are sold.

Anytime you have such profound changes in an industry, you will inevitably see new terminology, or jargon, arising. If you read the Red Sneaker newsletter on a regular basis, you may be familiar with most of these terms, but just in case, here are the ones I hear people ask about most frequently at WriterCon, cruises, and retreats.

1. **High concept books**: This term can seem particularly mysterious, in part because many people who use it can't explain it. The idea is that the "high concept" or premise is so distinctive that it not only describes the book but sells it. This might be an original idea, an inversion of the expected, or a fresh combination of successful elements. John Grisham's *The Firm* was pitched as "*L.A. Law* meets *The Godfather*"—and that worked out pretty well for him.

2. **Elevator pitch**: The elevator pitch works best when your book has a high concept and you know what it is. The idea is that your book can be described and sold in the time it takes to ride to the lobby in an elevator with an agent you've unexpectedly encountered—so no more than a sentence or two. Basically, this is an encapsulation of the premise or high concept. It is *not* a synopsis or plot description.

3. **Author platform**: This is a way of describing your ability to sell books based upon who you are or the people you are able to reach. It is *not* the same as your ability to market or pay for advertising. The most common measurement of author platform today is social media presence. How many Twitter followers do you have? Have many people see your author Facebook page? Do people read your reviews on Goodreads? Do you have a newsletter, blog, or podcast? Do you have mailing lists? Presumably you can reach these people and they will know and care when you release a new book.

4. **Sensitivity reads**: Inclusion is wonderful, but some writers have been derailed by Twitterstorms arising when someone decides they are not sufficiently sensitive to minority concerns. A sensitivity reader reviews projects for misrepresentations, bias, racism, or unintentional stereotypes. Presumably, the reader is someone who has the knowledge or experience to judge these matters. Unlike other editors, they will not proof, look for plotholes, or rewrite your prose. Instead, they will look for offensive content, misrepresentations, or similar potential problems.

5. **Developmental edit**: This edit should occur early in the writing process, possibly after the first reasonably coherent draft is finished. There's no point in nitpicking the language this early. This edit should focus on the structure of the story and the content. Does the story achieve its goals? Is it engaging? Are the

characters distinct? Does the plot make sense? Is the tone consistent? If you resist outside input, there's no point in asking for a developmental edit, but if you have an open mind, this can be invaluable.

6. **Line edit**: This edit focuses on the writing style and language. The goal is to improve the readability of the book. It is *not* the same as copyediting or proofreading. The goal is not to catch typos and boo-boos—that should come later—but to improve the way you use language to tell your story.

7. **Beta reader**: Someone the writer sends the manuscript to after it is substantially finished to receive input and guidance, particular on plot, pacing, consistency, and emotional impact.

8. **Big Five**: This term refers to the five largest traditional publishers feeding books into the American marketplace: Hachette, HarperCollins, Macmillan, Penguin Random House (the largest), and Simon & Schuster. Although all five have New York offices, only Simon & Schuster is American-owned. Before the digital revolution, these five corporations supplied abut 80% of the books in the American marketplace, but with the advent of eBooks, online sales, and self-publishing, that percentage has decreased dramatically.

9. **Traditional publishing**: A traditional publisher buys the right to publish your book, typically through a literary agent, and pays you a royalty in return. The publisher handles production, distribution, and marketing.

10. **Self-publishing** (or independent/indie publishing or artisanal publishing): Authors retain the rights to their work and serve as their own publisher, distributor, and marketer.

11. **Hybrid publishing**: Authors who have both traditional publishing contracts and also publish some of their own work.

12. **Vanity press**: Any entity that asks you to pay to be published. They may call it a "marketing fee" or a "distribution escrow" or anything else, but if the publisher asks you to pay them, it's a ripoff and you should refuse. Sadly, today many traditional publishers have distinct vanity-press lines. The gullible author can brag that they have a contract with a major publisher, but they really don't, and the book will not be marketed or distributed to any significant degree.

13. **Creative nonfiction**: A relatively new genre that blends fact and fiction. It typically employs literary devices and techniques and targets literary fiction readers more than nonfiction readers.

14. **Branding**: A known name or trademark that carries perceptions and expectations for readers. John Grisham's brand is legal thrillers (though he often writes other things). Stephen King's brand is horror (though he often writes other things).

15. **MSWL** (manuscript wish list): Shorthand typically used by agents on their webpages to describe what they want to see.

16. **Flash fiction**: Work that is extremely short and yet still tells a complete story. Seen more frequently as a contest category than in publications.

APPENDIX D: COMMONLY CONFUSED WORDS

Affect/Effect: Contrary to the commonly espoused rule, both words can be used as nouns and verbs, depending upon your meaning. *Affect* is usually a verb meaning "to have an effect on," but it can also be used to mean "countenance" or "emotion," as in, "The Vulcan had a flat affect." *Effect* is usually a noun meaning "impact" or "consequence," but it can also be used as a verb (a shortened form of "effectuate") meaning "to bring about."

Aggravate/Irritate: *Aggravate* means to worsen. *Irritate* means to inflame or anger. Many people use *aggravate* to mean "vex, annoy, or irritate," but that is not strictly speaking correct.

Allude/Refer: Yes, there is a difference. To *allude* is "to hint at or mention indirectly." To *refer* is "to mention directly." "Are you alluding to my height when you call me 'Napoleon?'" "You're short," she said, referring to his height.

Alternate/Alternative: *Alternate* means "one after the other." *Alternative* means "one instead of the other." Walking requires the *alternate* use of the left and right foot. The *alternative* is the bus.

Amused/Bemused: *Amused* means you're having a good time. *Bemused* means you're befuddled or puzzled or deep in thought.

Attorney General/Attorneys General: The plural of *attorney* *general* is *attorneys general,* as in: "Several assistant attorneys general appeared on behalf of the state." In this phrase, *general* is an adjective following the noun (a postpositive adjective), not a noun. The same is true of "Presidents Elect" or "mothers-in-law" or "passersby," but is not correct for a true compound word such as "spoonful." The plural would be "spoonfuls," not "spoonsful."

Besides/Beside: *Besides* means other than or in addition. *Beside* means alongside. "No one *besides* her son could stand so close beside her."

Big of a/Big of: As always, eliminate unnecessary words that add nothing to the sentence. Don't say, "How *big of a* case is it?" The same is true of "long of a" "slow of a" and other similar constructions.

Childlike/Childish: *Childish* is a pejorative adjective suggesting that someone is acting like a child and that isn't good. The positive way of saying the exact same thing is *childlike.*

Complement/Compliment: To *complement* is to complete or pair with or round out. To *compliment* is to praise.

Continuous/Continual: *Continuous* means uninterrupted. *Continual* means repeated, but intermittent. "Jack had to wind the grandfather clock continually to make it run continuously."

Convince/Persuade: You *convince* someone of something, but you *persuade* them to do something. *Convince* is usually followed by "that" or "of," but *persuade* is always followed by "to."

Corroborate/Collaborate: To *corroborate* evidence is to fortify it with additional evidence. To *collaborate* on a project is to work with someone else on it.

Could/Couldn't Care Less: If your intent is to say that you care as little as it is possible to care, use the phrase "couldn't care less." If you could care less, that means you already care at least a little.

Counsel/Council: *Counsel* means "advice," but it can also be a noun meaning "lawyer" or "consultant," in effect, a shortened form of "counselor." *Council* is a committee that leads or governs.

Credulous/Incredible: The *incredible* is unbelievable. Credulous people are gullible. *Incredulous* means you do not believe.

Datum/Data: *Datum* is the traditional singular, *data* the plural, but today, many people use *data* as a singular noun and few dictionaries or grammarians are still suggesting that it is incorrect.

Deserts/Desserts: In this example: What one deserves is one's *just deserts*. This use of *deserts* is related to the verb *deserve*. "The unsuccessful plaintiff got his just deserts." Deserts are dry, arid, sandy places, preferably in Cabo, and desserts include tiramisu and sopaipillas.

Discreet/Discrete: *Discreet* means "careful" or "prudent." *Discrete* means "separate, distinct, or unconnected." "Jack was *discreet* about his secret for maintaining two wives and two *discrete* households."

Disinterested/Uninterested: *Disinterested* means impartial or fair. *Uninterested* means not interested, bored, unengaged. "The judge was disinterested in the outcome of the case, and uninterested in the uncivil behavior of the divorce attorney."

Divorcé/Divorcée: *Divorcé* is for men, *divorcée* is for women.

Elicit/Illicit: To *elicit* is to evoke. *Illicit* means "illegal."

Emigrate/Immigrate: It's all about coming and going. You *emigrate* from a country and *immigrate* to another. For a mnemonic, remember that "exit" starts with an "e," like *"emigrate,"* and "in" starts with an "i," like *"immigrate."*

Eminent/Imminent/Immanent: *Eminent* means "famous or superior." *Imminent* means "impending." *Immanent* (rare these days, outside of the church) means "inherent or dwelling within."

Farther/Further: *Farther* refers to physical distance. *Further* means "to a greater extent or degree."

Fewer/Less: "Fewer" is used when the items in question can be counted. "Less" is used for items not subject to easy enumeration. "We had *fewer* writers than we'd hoped for, but *less* optimism than I expected." Obviously, the sign in every supermarket reading "Ten Items or Less" is just wrong.

Hadn't/Hadn't of: *"Hadn't of"* is ugly and grammatically incorrect.

Hanged/Hung: Murderers and horse thieves used to be *hanged.* "Hung" is incorrect in that context. But paintings and coats are *hung.*

Historic/Historical: *Historic* means "having a place in history." *Historical* means "pertaining to the subject of history."

Home in/Hone in: "We need to *home* in on the precise problem."

Imply/Infer: To imply means to suggest something. To infer means to conclude from available evidence. Speakers imply. Listeners infer. Writers imply. Readers infer. "You imply that I'm a moron," the husband said. "You infer correctly," the wife replied.

Ingenuous/Ingenious: *Ingenuous* means naïve, frank, or candid, coming from the same root word as "ingénue." *Ingenious* means crafty. Disingenuous means dishonest.

It's/Its: *It's* is the contraction for *it is. Its* is a possessive pronoun.

Jones's/Joneses: One guy is a *Jones,* but the whole family are the *Joneses.* If you are discussing something they own, that would be the *Joneses'.* The same is true of other family names ending in "s."

Laudable/Laudatory: *Laudable* means praiseworthy. *Laudatory* means praiseful. "He did a laudable job of reading the laudatory psalms."

Lie/Lay: *Lie* means to recline. The simple past tense of *lie* is *lay* and the past participle is *lain.* Lay can also be a verb indicating placement, and therein lies the confusion. The past tense of *lay* is *laid.* "Today you *lie* in the same bed where I lay my car keys."

Memoranda/Memorandum: *Memoranda* is plural, *memorandum* is singular.

Neither/Nor: Whether the verb in a "neither/nor" sentence is singular or plural depends upon the second element. Therefore, "Neither you nor I *am* responsible," but, "Neither I nor they *are* responsible." "Neither" by itself means by implication "neither one," so it takes a singular verb, as in, "Neither of your objections *is* correct." The same is true for "either," as in: "Either the plaintiff or one of the other lawyers *is* responsible for the judge's verdict."

Number/Amounts: Countable items have a *number*. Non-countable items are measured in *amounts*.

Overflowed/Overflow: *Overflowed* is the past tense and past participle of the verb *overflow*.

Persecute/Prosecute: To *persecute* is to torment. To *prosecute* is to conduct criminal proceedings. "The defendant felt *persecuted* when the DA *prosecuted* him the second time."

Principal/Principle: *Principal* means "main or primary." *Principle* means "rule or standard." "The school principal said his principal goal was to reinvest the trust fund principal, as a matter of principle."

Prophesy/Prophecy: *Prophesy* is a verb meaning "to foretell." *Prophecy* is a noun indicating what was foretold. "Madame Martel dropped her fee per prophecy, because she could prophesy a downturn in the economy."

Prospective/Perspective: *Prospective* means "potential." *Perspective* means "viewpoint."

Ravage/Ravish: A famous headline in a Minnesota newspaper read: "Queen Elizabeth Ravished." As you might have guessed, the ocean liner *Queen Elizabeth* caught fire and burned, and the paper should have said "Queen Elizabeth Ravaged" (though that sill doesn't sound very good). *Ravaged* means "damaged or destroyed." *Ravished* means "carried away (by force or by emotion) or sexually assaulted." When you say that your sweetheart looked *ravishing*, you're not implying a desire to do anything illegal. You're saying the sight of her swept you away with emotion.

Regardless/Irregardless: *Irregardless* is still considered substandard by most authorities, though it technically has the same meaning as "regardless."

Regretful/Regrettable: *Regretful* means "full of regret." *Regrettable* means "unfortunate, a cause for regret." "Florence *regretfully* swept up the pieces of the Ming vase she had *regrettably* smashed."

Reigned/Reined: "The legal fees when Queen Elizabeth reigned had to be *reined* in by the Privy Council."

Reluctant/Reticent: Although people often use these as synonyms, their true meanings aren't even similar. *Reluctant* means unwilling, but *reticent* means silent. "The *reluctant* witness was *reticent* on the witness stand."

Stationer/Stationery/Stationary: A *stationer* sells *stationery* (a good mnemonic device is to recall that there is an *"er"* in *"paper"*). *Stationary* objects (like stationery) do not move.

Stolen/Robbed: Money and other things of value are *stolen*. People, places, and businesses are *robbed*.

Therefore/Therefor: *Therefore* means "accordingly" or "in conclusion." *Therefor* is an ugly and archaic piece of legalese meaning "for it" or "for them," as in, "He bought a bicycle and paid *therefor*."

Tortuous/Torturous: *Tortuous* means "winding or crooked or twisty." *Torturous* means "painful." "During the tortuous drive, Jack developed a torturous ache in his backside."

Who/Whom: Most modern grammarians now say "who" can always be used in place of "whom" at the beginning of a sentence or clause. "Whom" should still be used after a preposition. So "Who from?" is correct, but so is "From whom?" Most American lexicographers, from Daniel Webster on down, have argued for clarifying the confusion by eliminating "whom" altogether, but it hasn't happened yet.

Whose/Who's: *Whose* is the possessive relative pronoun. *Who's* is the contraction for *who is*. "*Who's* the person for *whose* benefit the trust fund was established?"

APPENDIX E: REVISION CHECKLIST

I s there a reason to care about these characters?

Does the motivation deepen as the story progresses? Do the stakes increase?

Is there tension on every page? Does the tension start with the first sentence?

Are descriptive details and dialogue voice unique to each major character?

Are there too many similar scenes in a row?

Does the pace slow at any point?

How many emotional triggers have you put into place? How will they affect the reader?

Does your protagonist demonstrate a sympathetic or empathetic quality in the first five pages?

Do the plot complications increase as the story progresses?

What is extraordinary about this character or world or plot you've created?

Does the story culminate in a climax that is satisfying, dramatic, suspenseful, and unexpected?

Does the story have a denouement that resolves remaining plot points, subplots, or character arcs?

Have you said what you wanted to say with this story?

APPENDIX F: DIALOGUE CHECKLIST

Here's a shortlist of the characteristics of dynamic, memorable dialogue, followed by a list of the faults most commonly found in poor dialogue.

Great Dialogue...

Imparts a sense of realism (without necessarily being realistic)

Reveals character

Advances the story

Suggests what is not being said

Reveals hidden motivations

Reflects the characters' history (or perhaps baggage)

Reflects the hierarchal relationship between the person speaking and the person or persons listening

Refers back to something said earlier

Foreshadows what is yet to come

Has a purpose

Has emotional impact

Is memorable or even quotable

And poor dialogue...

Sounds artificial, stiff, or wooden

Seems stilted or unnatural

Contains too much exposition

Is too on-the-nose

Only conveys the obvious, or what the reader already knows

Has all the characters sounding alike

Has characters calling each other by name too often

Has too many conversational stutters, slang terms, colloqui-alisms, or pointless chitchat

Conveys dialect or foreign languages phonetically

Contains unnecessary attributions

Uses attributions or stage directions to convey emotional information that should be imbedded in the dialogue itself

Is riddled with exclamation points

Is riddled with profanity

Uses synonyms and substitutes for "said" to no good purpose

Is dull circular, or monotonous

APPENDIX G: FIRST PAGES

The first page is what gets you published...

1. Always think of the reader (not your friends, spouse, editor, agent, critique group).

2. How long will readers continue reading if they're not engaged in the story?

3. Start with something that captures the reader's interest. Doesn't have to be a shotgun blast. Just seize their attention. Pose unanswered questions. No weather reports. No landscape. No exposition. No backstory. No infodumps.

4. Go to the bookstore and read the first pages of the "New Releases."

5. Great openings all have this in common: directness, something that pulls the reader into the story, and something that suggests a great reading experience lies ahead.

6. Once you have crafted an opening sentence that accomplishes all this, try to maintain the same tone throughout the first page. Then the first chapter. Then the entire book.

My Favorite Openings:

"It is a truth universally acknowledged that a single man in possession of a good fortune must be in want of a wife."
   Jane Austin, *Pride and Prejudice*

"It was a pleasure to burn."
   Ray Bradbury, *Fahrenheit 451*

"Many years later, as he faced the firing squad, Colonel Aureliano Buendia was to remember that distant afternoon when his father took him to discover ice."
   G. G. Marquez, *One Hundred Years of Solitude*

"Fog everywhere. Fog up the river, where it flows among green aits and meadows; fog down the river, where it rolls defiled among the tiers of shipping, and the waterside pollutions of a great (and dirty) city."
   Charles Dickens, *Bleak House*

"Sitting beside the road, watching the wagon mount the hill toward her, Lena thinks, 'I have come from Alabama: a fur piece. All the way from Alabama a-walking. A fur piece.' Thinking although I have not been quite a month on the road I am already in Mississippi, further from home than I have ever been before. I am now further from Doane's Mill than I have been since I was twelve years old"
   William Faulkner, *Light in August*

"I died three days ago."

W. Bernhardt, *Capitol Offense*

"Once again," the man said, pulling the little girl along by the leash tied to his wrist and hers. "Tell me your name."

W. Bernhardt, *Primary Justice*

"'Take my camel, dear,'" said my Aunt Dot, as she climbed down from this animal on her return from High Mass."

Rose Macaulay, *Towers of Trebizond*

"Dr. Weiss, at forty, knew that her life had been ruined by literature."

Anita Brookner, *The Debut*

"I was not sorry when my brother died."

Tsitsi Dangarembga, *Nervous Conditions*

"If I could tell you one thing about my life it would be this: when I was seven years old the mailman ran over my head."

Brady Udall, *The Miracle Life of Edgar Mint*

"First I had to get his body into the boat."

Rhian Ellis, *After Life*

"I joined the baboon troop during my twenty-first year. I had never planned to become a savanna baboon when I grew up; instead, I had always assumed I would become a mountain gorilla."

Robert Sapoisky, *A Primate's Memoir*

"Atlas Malone saw the angel again, this time down by the horse chestnut tree."

Jon Cohen, *The Man in the Window*

"When I finally caught up with Abraham Trehearne, he was drinking beer with an alcoholic bulldog named Fireball Roberts in a ramshackle joint just outside of Sonoma, California, drinking the heart right out of a fine spring morning."

James Crumley, *The Last Good Kiss*

"Over the weekend the vultures got into the presidential palace by pecking through the screens on the balcony windows and the flapping of their wings stirred up the stagnant time inside, and at dawn on Monday the city awoke out of its lethargy of centuries with the warm, soft breeze of a great man dead and rotting grandeur."

Gabriel Garcia Marquez, *The Autumn of the Patriarch*

APPENDIX H: MEMORABLE PIECES OF PROSE

I would be willing to bet that none of these great bits of writing emerged during the first draft. This level of excellence only comes from a writer working hard and revising until the work is as good as it can possibly be.

IT WAS THE BEST OF TIMES, IT WAS THE WORST OF TIMES, IT WAS THE age of wisdom, it was the age of foolishness, it was the epoch of belief, it was the epoch of incredulity, it was the season of Light, it was the season of Darkness, it was the spring of hope, it was the winter of despair, we had everything before us, we had nothing before us, we were all going direct to Heaven, we were all going direct the other way – in short, the period was so far like the present period, that some of its noisiest authorities insisted on its being received, for good or for evil, in the superlative degree of comparison only. —Charles Dickens, *A Tale of Two Cities*

FATE IS LIKE A STRANGE, UNPOPULAR RESTAURANT, FILLED WITH

odd waiters who bring you things you never asked for and don't always like. —Lemony Snicket

LIFE ISN'T ABOUT WHAT HAPPENS TO YOU, IT'S ABOUT HOW YOU handle what happens. —Nicholas Evans, *The Smoke Jumper*

DEATH IS BUT THE NEXT GREAT ADVENTURE. —ALBUS Dumbledore (J.K. Rowling) (*Harry Potter and the Sorcerer's Stone*)

AND I, OF COURSE, AM INNOCENT OF ALL BUT MALICE. —FIONA, *Sign of the Unicorn*, Roger Zelazny

AND IF YOU'RE GOING TO CRITICIZE ME FOR NOT FINISHING THE whole thing and tying it up in a bow for you, why, do us both a favor and write your own damn book.... —Orson Scott Card, *Alvin Journeyman*

BECAUSE WE ARE THE PEOPLE, AND THE PEOPLE GO ON. —MA JOAD, *The Grapes of Wrath*, John Steinbeck

DEATH BELONGS TO GOD ALONE. BY WHAT RIGHT DO MEN TOUCH that unknown thing? —Victor Hugo, *Les Misérables*

LIFE IS A GIFT HORSE. —J.D. SALINGER, *TEDDY*

. . .

LIFE IS PAIN. ANYBODY THAT SAYS DIFFERENT IS SELLING something. —Fezzik's mother, *The Princess Bride*

NOT ALL WHO WANDER ARE LOST. —J.R.R. TOLKIEN, *THE Fellowship of the Ring*

THE SUREST SIGN THAT THERE IS INTELLIGENT LIFE ELSEWHERE IN the universe is that none of it has tried to contact us. —*Calvin and Hobbes*

A BORE IS A PERSON WHO DEPRIVES YOU OF SOLITUDE WITHOUT providing you with company. —John MacDonald, *The Turquoise Lament*

ALL ANIMALS ARE EQUAL, BUT SOME ARE MORE EQUAL THAN others. —George Orwell, *Animal Farm*

BEHIND THEM LAY PAIN, AND DEATH, AND FEAR. AHEAD OF THEM lay doubt, and danger, and fathomless mysteries. But they weren't alone. —Philip Pullman, *The Golden Compass*

CERTAIN THINGS SHOULD JUST STAY AS THEY ARE. YOU OUGHT TO be able to stick them in one of those big glass cases and just leave them alone. —JD Salinger, *Catcher in the Rye*

DAD, HOW DO SOLDIERS KILLING EACH OTHER SOLVE THE WORLD'S problems? —*Calvin and Hobbes*

APPENDIX I: THE RED SNEAKER
WRITER'S READING LIST

The Chicago Manual of Style. 16th ed. Chicago: University of Chicago Press, 2010.

Cook, Vivian. *All in a Word: 100 Delightful Excursions into the Uses and Abuses of Words*. Brooklyn: Melville House, 2010.

Fowler, H.W. *Fowler's Modern English Usage*. 3rd ed. Rev. Ernest Gowers. N.Y. & Oxford: Oxford University Press, 2004.

Goldman, William. *Adventures in the Screen Trade: A Personal View of Hollywood and Screenwriting*. New York: Grand Central, 1989.

Hale, Constance. *Sin and Syntax: How to Create Wickedly Effective Prose*. New York: Broadway Books, 2001.

Hart, Jack. *A Writer's Coach: The Complete Guide to Writing Strategies That Work*. New York: Anchor Books, 2006.

Jones, Catherine Ann. *The Way of Story: The Craft and Soul of Writing*. Studio City: Michael Wiese Productions, 2007.

Klauser, Henriette Anne. *Writing on Both Sides of the Brain*. San Francisco: Harper & Row, 1987.

Maass, Donald. *The Fire in Fiction: Passion, Purpose, and Techniques to Make Your Novel Great*. Cincinnati: Writers Digest Books, 2009.

Maass, Donald. *Writing the Breakout Novel: Insider Advice for Taking Your Fiction to the Next Level*. Cincinnati: Writers Digest Books, 2001.

Maass, Donald. *Writing 21st Century Fiction: High Impact Techniques for Exceptional Storytelling*. Cincinnati: Writers Digest Books, 2012.

O'Conner, Patricia T. *Woe Is I: The Grammarphobe's Guide to Better English in Plain English*. 2nd ed. New York: Riverhead Books, 2003.

O'Conner, Patricia T. *Origins of the Specious: Myths and Misconceptions of the English Language*. New York: Random House, 2009.

Strunk, William, Jr., and White, E.B. *The Elements of Style*. 4th ed. N.Y.: Macmillan, 2000.

Truss, Lynne. *Eats Shoots & Leaves: The Zero Tolerance Guide to Punctuation*. New York: Gotham Books, 2005.

Vogler, Christopher. *The Writer's Journey: Mythic Structure for Storytellers and Screenwriters*. Studio City: Michael Wiese Productions, 1992.

Zinsler, William. *On Writing Well: The Classic Guide to Writing Nonfiction*. 30th Anniv. Ed. New York: Harper Perennial, 2006.

ABOUT THE AUTHOR

William Bernhardt is the author of over fifty books, including *The Last Chance Lawyer (Amazon #1 Bestseller)*, the historical novels *Challengers of the Dust* and *Nemesis*, two books of poetry, and the Red Sneaker books on fiction writing. In addition, Bernhardt founded the Red Sneaker Writers Center to mentor aspiring authors. The Center hosts an annual conference (WriterCon), small-group seminars, a newsletter, a phone app, and a bi-weekly podcast. He is also the owner of Balkan Press, which publishes poetry and fiction as well as the literary journal *Conclave*.

Bernhardt has received the Southern Writers Guild's Gold Medal Award, the Royden B. Davis Distinguished Author Award (University of Pennsylvania) and the H. Louise Cobb Distinguished Author Award (Oklahoma State), which is given "in recognition of an outstanding body of work that has profoundly influenced the way in which we understand ourselves and American society at large." In 2019, he received the Arrell Gibson Lifetime Achievement Award from the Oklahoma Center for the Book.

In addition Bernhardt has written plays, a musical (book and score), humor, children's stories, biography, and puzzles. He has edited two anthologies (*Legal Briefs* and *Natural Suspect*) as fundraisers for The Nature Conservancy and the Children's Legal Defense Fund. In his spare time, he has enjoyed surfing, digging for dinosaurs, trekking through the Himalayas, paragliding, scuba diving, caving, zip-lining over the canopy of the Costa Rican rain forest, and jumping out of an airplane at 10,000 feet.

In 2017, when Bernhardt delivered the keynote address at the

San Francisco Writers Conference, chairman Michael Larsen noted that in addition to penning novels, Bernhardt can "write a sonnet, play a sonata, plant a garden, try a lawsuit, teach a class, cook a gourmet meal, beat you at Scrabble, and work the *New York Times* crossword in under five minutes."

For more information
www.williambernhardt.com
wb@williambernhardt.com

AUTHOR'S NOTE

Watch for the next volume in the Red Sneaker Writers Book series.

Would you consider posting a review of this book online? I'd really appreciate it. I hope you'll also consider reading some of my fiction, including the Daniel Pike novels, starting with *The Last Chance Lawyer*.

Please consider attending WriterCon over Labor Day weekend in Oklahoma City. For more information, visit www.writercon.org. If you're interested in attending one of my small-group writing retreats, visit my webpage.

Need some feedback on your writing? Check out my Patreon page at https://www.patreon.com/willbern

I publish a free e-newsletter on a regular basis. The Red Sneaker Writers Newsletter is for writers and aspiring writers, filled with market and writing news. You can sign up at my website. There's also a bi-weekly Red Sneakers podcast, available everywhere you get podcasts.

For more information, please visit my website at http://www.williambernhardt.com. You can email me at willbern@gmail.com.

Made in the USA
Coppell, TX
29 April 2025

48815097R10073